AS LEVEL

Business Studies

Examination Handbook

Andrew Gillespie

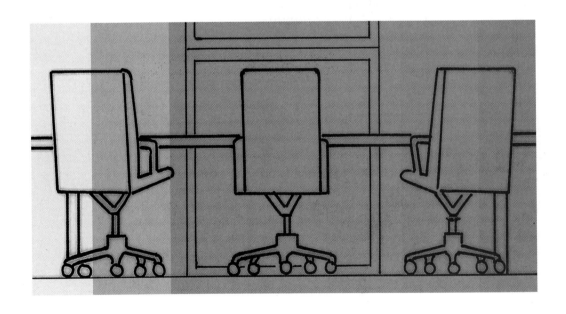

OXFORD

UNIVERSITY PRESS

OXFORD
UNIVERSITY PRESS

Great Clarendon Street, Oxford OX2 6DP

Oxford University Press is a department of the University of Oxford.
It furthers the University's objective of excellence in research, scholarship, and
education by publishing worldwide in

Oxford   New York

Auckland   Bangkok   Buenos Aires   Cape Town   Chennai
Dar es Salaam   Delhi   Hong Kong   Istanbul   Karachi   Kolkata
Kuala Lumpur   Madrid   Melbourne   Mexico City   Mumbai   Nairobi
São Paulo   Shanghai   Taipei   Tokyo   Toronto

Oxford is a registered trade mark of Oxford University Press
in the UK and in certain other countries

© Andrew Gillespie 2002

Database right Oxford University Press (maker)

First published 2002

British Library Cataloguing in Publication Data

Data available

ISBN 0 19 832843 5

10 9 8 7 6 5 4 3 2 1

Typeset by TechSet Ltd, Gateshead, Tyne and Wear.
Printed in Great Britain.

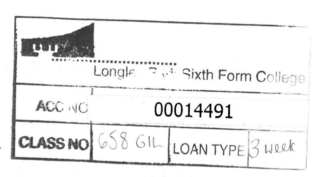

Contents

Your route to AS-Level exam success

This handbook will help you to study more effectively and will help you to develop the key skills – understanding, application, analysis and evaluation – to improve your exam grades significantly. You can use it to check your progress throughout your course and as an essential part of your revision in the build-up to the exams.

The *AS Business Studies Exam Handbook* covers all the areas of the AS-Level specification for the main examination boards.

The book is divided into units, each covering a particular topic. Each unit is broken down into:

- Content list – key points and terms that you need to know.
- Analysis list – suggested analysis of key points in the topic.
- Evaluation list – suggested evaluation of key points in the topic.
- Examiner's advice on answering exam questions on the topic.
- Maths section – the techniques you need to know for the topic. (*Note:* some topics do not have maths questions.)
- Practice questions – maths questions, diagram questions and quick questions to test yourself (answers at the back of the book).
- Marking exam answers – a student's answer marked by a senior examiner with comments, and a chance for you to mark a student's answer and compare your marks with an examiner's.

At the end of the book, four tests on the whole specification allow you to check how well you know the topics and identify those that need more revision. Six review tests contain more questions on the main areas of the specification.

Good luck in your exams!
Andrew Gillespie

Skills for success at AS-Level Business Studies

To succeed at AS-Level Business Studies you need to demonstrate the following skills.

- **Content/knowledge**

  You will be asked to demonstrate your "knowledge" of the terms and concepts in the subject. You may be asked for definitions and equations or to identify relevant factors in a given situation. The "content" section in each unit provides a brief summary of the knowledge you are likely to need in the exam.

- **Explanation/application**

  As well as knowing what particular terms and words mean, you need to be able to explain and show what they mean. The questions you are asked in the exam will usually be based on a given situation or a case study. To gain marks you should relate any points you make to this particular business situation. This is called "application". There is more advice on application, starting on page x.

- **Analysis**

  Analysis involves examining your arguments in more depth. For example, as well as explaining what some of your points mean, you may need to show why they are significant. There is more advice on analysis, starting on page xi.

- **Evaluation**

  To demonstrate this skill you need to show judgement in your answer. For example, you may weigh up two sides of the argument and come to a conclusion about which side is the stronger. Or you may analyse three important factors in an answer and then consider which one is most important. Alternatively you may simply make a judgement about the actions a particular firm would take in the given situation. There is more advice on evaluation, starting on page xiii.

Skills hierarchy

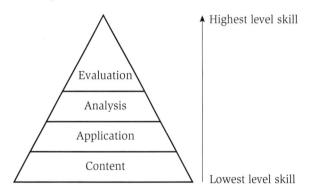

Content is the lowest level skill. It simply involves learning the material (hard work, but not too complicated).

As you go up the hierarchy, the skills become more challenging.

First you have to **apply** your ideas, then develop the argument (**analyse**) and finally show judgement (**evaluation**). Evaluation is the most difficult skill, because it involves "standing back" from your arguments and reflecting on their relative importance.

Which skills are needed when

At some point in your exams you need to demonstrate all four skills. However, you do not need to show all of them all the time. Part of the skill of preparing for the exam is knowing exactly what you need to do for each paper and each type of question.

For example, if a question asks you to "State two ways of measuring market size" this is a very basic question. You only need to demonstrate knowledge (**content**) and you do not have to write much to get the marks. (For example, "The size of a market can be measured by the value of the sales and by the volume of sales.").

On the other hand, if the question asks "To what extent should a firm invest in training?" this requires a discussion of the case for and against investing and some judgement (**evaluation**).

Matching the right skill to the question is a vital part of exam technique. The table below should help you to recognise the skills required for different types of question.

Trigger word	Highest skill needed
State	Content
Identify	Content
Explain	Explanation/application
Examine	Analysis
Analyse	Analysis
Discuss	Evaluation
To what extent	Evaluation

Whatever the type of question, at AS-Level it is useful to define the term or concept being examined. By defining your terms accurately you immediately demonstrate your understanding of the topic. For example, for the question "Discuss the benefits of delegation" you could begin your answer by defining "delegation".

To do well in the exams you also need a complete understanding of each paper you will be taking: how long it lasts and exactly what will be assessed. For more details on the AQA, OCR and Edexcel exams, see pages vi (below) to ix.

How questions are marked in the exam

All exam boards use a "levels of response" approach to marking. This means that the quality of your argument is more important than the number of points you make. The better the quality of your argument, the higher the level you reach and the more marks you get. This means that it is better to analyse two points effectively rather than analyse several points weakly. So in an exam, make sure you concentrate on demonstrating a particular skill well, rather than simply demonstrating the skill many times over.

The *Marking exam questions* sections in the units allow you to see how an examiner has marked a student's answer and then try marking an answer yourself. This gives you a greater understanding of how the marking scheme works and what the examiner is looking for, which will help you when you write your own answers.

Although the marking approach is generally the same for all the exam boards, the way in which it is implemented does differ a little, as shown below.

AQA AS-Level Business Studies

In the AQA exams, the different skills are marked separately. For example, in a question that requires analysis you will get a mark for **content**, another mark for **application** and another one for **analysis**. These three marks are added together to give the total.

A mark scheme for a 7 mark question requiring analysis.

Level	Content 2 marks	Application 2 marks	Analysis 3 marks
Level 2	2 marks Good understanding demonstrated	2 marks Good application demonstrated	3-2 marks Good analysis demonstrated
Level 1	1 mark Limited understanding demonstrated	1 mark Limited application demonstrated	1 mark Limited analysis demonstrated
Level 0	0 marks No understanding demonstrated	0 marks No application demonstrated	0 marks No analysis demonstrated

There are three levels of response for each skill. Good quality content, application or analysis reaches a higher level than poor quality content, application or analysis. Notice that you must demonstrate *each* of the skills to achieve the full marks.

For questions requiring evaluation, the approach is similar.

A mark scheme for a 10 mark question requiring evaluation.

Level	Content 2 marks	Application 2 marks	Analysis 3 marks	Evaluation 3 marks
Level 2	2 marks Good understanding demonstrated	2 marks Good application demonstrated	3-2 marks Good analysis demonstrated	3-2 marks Good judgement demonstrated
Level 1	1 mark Limited understanding demonstrated	1 mark Limited application demonstrated	1 mark Limited analysis demonstrated	1 mark Limited judgement demonstrated
Level 0	0 marks No understanding demonstrated	0 marks No application demonstrated	0 marks No analysis demonstrated	0 marks No judgement demonstrated

So to succeed in AQA exams you need:

■ To be able to recognise which skills are required in particular questions.
■ To demonstrate each of the appropriate skills.

OCR and Edexcel AS-Level Business Studies

The OCR and Edexcel marking approach does not give separate marks for each skill. It gives one overall mark for the question, based on the skills demonstrated and the quality of the skill shown.

Here is a typical OCR mark scheme:

Level 4	Answer demonstrates evaluation	15-11 marks
Level 3	Answer demonstrates analysis	10-7 marks
Level 2	Answer demonstrates understanding of concepts involved in context	6-4 marks
Level 1	Answer identifies appropriate concepts and issues	3-1 marks

The higher the skill demonstrated, the higher the level you achieve. An answer that analyses superbly can only achieve 10 marks. However, an answer that evaluates (however weakly) can achieve 11 marks.

To do well in an OCR or Edexcel examination you need:

■ To identify the highest skills required for each question.
■ To demonstrate that skill in your answer.

AS-Level Business Studies exam specifications

AQA exam specification

Unit 1: Marketing and finance

A 1-hour paper containing two questions based on relatively short data material (for example, an extract from a newspaper article).

One question is mainly on marketing topics. One question is mainly on finance topics. Each question is worth 25 marks.

In each 25-mark question, evaluation is only tested in the final part.

Unit 2 People and operations

Unit 3 Business objectives and strategy and external influences

Units 2 and 3 are assessed via a pre-seen case study covering people, operations, objectives and strategy, and external influences. There are two separate sets of questions on the case study (1 hour per set). Candidates may:

- *Either* take Units 2 and 3 at the same time (1 hour each)
- *Or* take either Unit 2 or Unit 3 on its own as a 1-hour paper

Both units 2 and have a total of 50 marks.

Breakdown of skills required for each AQA paper

	Knowledge %	Application %	Analysis %	Evaluation %
Unit 1	33.3	33.3	23.3	10
Unit 2	28.5	28.5	24	19
Unit 3	28.5	28.5	24	19

OCR exam specification

Unit	Name	Duration	Format	Weighting of AS
2871	Businesses, their objectives and environment	1 hour	A pre-seen case study	30%
2872	Business decisions	45 minutes	A single data response question subdivided into shorter elements	30%
2873	Business behaviour	1 hour 15 minutes	A pre-seen case study	40%

Overall assessment objectives for the OCR exam

Knowledge	Application	Analysis	Evaluation
30%	26.5%	23.5%	20%

Mark allocation for each OCR paper

Unit	Knowledge	Application	Analysis	Evaluation	Quality of written communication	Total marks
2871	13	12	10	8	2	45
2872	13	12	10	8	2	45
2873	17	15	14	12	2	60
TOTAL	**43**	**39**	**34**	**28**	**6**	**150**

Edexcel exam specification

Unit	Duration	Format	Weighting of AS
Unit 1 Business structures, objectives and external influences	1 hour	A pre-seen case study; 3 compulsory questions with subsections	30%
Unit 2 Marketing and production	1 hour	A pre-seen case study; 3 compulsory questions with subsections	30%
Unit 3 Financial management	1 hour	A pre-seen case study; 2 compulsory questions with subsections	40%

The pre-seen case study contains material for all three units (although students do not need to take all three units at one time).

Breakdown of skills required for each Edexcel paper

Unit	Knowledge %	Application %	Analysis %	Evaluation %
1	30	30	20	20
2	30	30	20	20
3	25	25	25	25

Demonstrating higher level skills

Application

When answering exam questions it is very important to *apply* your knowledge. This means that you should try and place your answer in context. Is it a small business or a big one? Does it manufacture goods or provide a service? Is it growing fast or in decline? These are all factors that you may consider when writing an answer. Good application refers closely to the type of business given in the question.

Compare the following two answers to this question:

Question

Explain the factors that might determine the price of a new car.

Answer A

The price may be affected by costs, because to make a profit you need to cover costs. It may also be affected by demand, because if you charge too much there may not be enough demand to make the product viable.

Answer B

The price of a new car may be determined by the costs of production, for example the costs of the metal, the windscreen, the tyres and the overall costs of running the production line. Obviously, to keep in business the price will have to cover the unit cost in the long run.

A firm may also consider competitors' models and their prices. If this car is seen as similar to some competitors' models then this needs to be taken into account, because customers may switch easily between the two. However the firm may believe it has special features such as the brand name (BMW or Jaguar), or the design or the engine specifications, that enable it to charge a relatively high price.

> ### Examiner's comment
> Answer B demonstrates application in the references to setting the price of a car. The candidate is thinking carefully about this industry. Answer A shows a general grasp of the issues but the answer could be about any product – it is not applied to the situation.

Now look at the answer to this question:

Question

Andros sells office equipment to small businesses. Its managing director wants to widen the range of products and has decided to undertake some market research. Explain one type of market research the firm might use.

Answer

Market research involves gathering and analysing information relevant to a firm's marketing activities. This may be primary (gathering information for the first time) or secondary (using existing information). For example, the firm could ask people in the street what they think, which is primary. It obviously could not ask everyone so it would need to take a sample. A sample is selected to represent the population as a whole. Primary research is up-to-date and specific to the needs of the business.

Now look at the answer to this question:

Question
How important is the price in the marketing of newspapers?

Answer
Marketing depends on the marketing mix – the 4Ps: Price, Place, Promotion and Product.

The Price cannot be too high or you will not sell anything at all.

Promotion is important because people must know that the product exists. Advertising is important here and so to sell newspapers you need to advertise.

Place also matters because you need to need to distribute them

The Product matters because it needs to last a long time, be durable and be reliable.

Analysis

Analysis is when an idea is developed or examined in depth.

Analysing includes:

- Showing why an idea matters. Very often students explain a point but do not then show why this is significant. Analysis takes the argument a step further.

  (1) "A piecework payment system may encourage staff to work harder because it links earnings to output."
  This does not fully develop the argument.

  (2) "A piecework payment system may encourage staff to work harder because it links earnings to output and therefore the more people produce, the more they will earn."
  This completes the chain of reasoning.

- Applying theory to the argument, by relating the argument to a business concept. For example, when considering a price change you might consider its impact using the price elasticity of demand.

  (1) "When you put the price up sales fall a lot"

  (2) "An increase in price is likely to lead to a fall in sales; the extent of the fall will depend on the price elasticity of demand. The more price elastic demand is, the greater the fall in sales."

  Answer (2) is a lot stronger because it makes use of business theory.

Using "therefore"

Although there is no set way of analysing, using "therefore" in your answers can help you to develop a logical chain of argument.

For example:

(1) "Delegating authority may motivate staff because they have the ability to make decisions for themselves and *therefore* productivity may increase."

(2) "A lean production approach may cut costs because it involves less waste and *therefore* this might lead to higher profit margins."

Now look at the following question and answer to see how "therefore" can be used.

Question

Analyse two possible benefits of market research to a restaurant.　　　　**(8 marks)**

Marked answer

Market research should increase the chance of a restaurant succeeding. (**Content**) This is because it will give the restaurant more information about its customers (**Explanation**) and *therefore* it can target its marketing activities more accurately and not waste resources (**Analysis**). For example, it can ask existing customers what they would like on the menu and *therefore* adjust this accordingly to increase their satisfaction. It could also ask people who do not come why they do not and *therefore* it will be able to see if it can change these things (for example, the price of the food) to attract more customers. (**Application & Analysis**)

> ### Examiner's comment
> This is a simple example of analysis. The student identifies a benefit of market research and explains why it is a benefit. She then develops this in context (by referring to menus and food prices), showing why this will provide an advantage for the firm.

Analysing data

Some questions will involve analysing data. For example, you might be told that a firm's productivity this year is +3%. To analyse this figure you could:

- **Examine the significance of the number** – for example, it may have an impact on the cost per unit and therefore a firm's profitability.

- **Examine the reasons why this number has occurred** – in this case, why productivity has increased. (For example, because of training or investment in technology.)

- **Compare this figure with others** – for example, is this productivity figure higher or lower than a competitor's? Or the past? If so, why?
- **Consider the context** – what figure would you have expected for this industry? Or what figure would management have expected?

Example

The number of staff leaving a firm has increased from 5% p.a. to 25% p.a.

What could be the reasons for this?

What could be the consequences of this increase in labour turnover?

Reasons for the increase in labour turnover may include:
- There has been a change in management style which is not welcomed by the staff and therefore they are looking for other work.
- A competitor is offering better pay for similar jobs and therefore staff are leaving to benefit from the higher rewards.

The consequences of an increase in labour turnover may be:
- There may be an increase in costs because staff have to be replaced and therefore recruitment costs are likely to increase.
- The firm may find it difficult to attract staff because they will hear that so many others are leaving; therefore the firm may face staff shortages.

You could also consider:
- The labour turnover rates of competitors – is this firm any different from its rivals?
- The industry. Some industries, such as fast-food restaurants, typically have high labour turnover. Provided the firm is prepared for this and there is a sufficient pool of labour, this may not be a problem.
- The time period involved. After Christmas, for example, a retailer's labour turnover may be very high because the firm may have used a lot of temporary labour over the holiday period to meet the demand.

In numerical questions you may be asked to calculate something first and then comment on your findings. Make sure you learn equations and how to use them.

You also need to be able to discuss the significance of your findings. What if break-even has increased for example? What if the labour turnover is 50%? What if inflation is 18%? You need to think about the size of numbers you might expect in different situations and the possible consequences if they are higher or lower than this.

So to analyse data:
- Consider the meaning of the value – what does it actually show?
- Consider the cause, the context and consequences.
- Compare with others or the past.

Evaluation

Evaluation involves judgement. You need to show that you really are thinking about your answer. Evaluation involves some consideration of what really matters in an argument, or a discussion of the most important factor.

There is no easy way of learning how to evaluate. You have to stand back from your answer and think about what makes a particular point or argument more or less important.

Ways of demonstrating evaluation include:

■ Develop two sides of an argument ("for" and "against") and then decide which side is the stronger (and why).

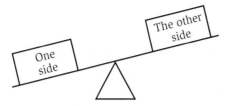

Analyse the two sides of the argument and then evaluate by weighing up the two sides and deciding which one is more significant.

■ Identify three important issues in an argument and then decide which one is the most significant.

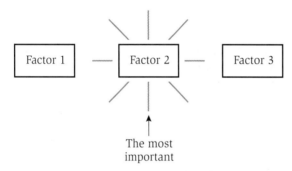

Analyse three different factors in an argument and evaluate by deciding which is the most important.

■ Think about the particular market in which a firm operates and comment on the most important features in *this* type of business environment, or why *this* firm might act in a particular way.

Phrases to use in evaluating include:

■ "*Overall* the way in which a firm will benefit depends on X because …"

■ "*In this situation,* factor Z is likely to be *most* important because …."

■ "For a firm such as Q, the *most likely* reaction is … because …"

■ "*In the short run* the firm is likely to do X because … However, in the long run …"

Notice how evaluation involves explanation. It is not enough to identify the most important factor, the most likely reaction, the key issue, the main reason and so on. You have to justify your answer – show why you think this is the most relevant, most significant, most important, …

Using "it depends"
To evaluate well you have to realise that there are no fixed answers in business – it depends. For example:

■ Whether a firm should put the price up or down *depends* on factors such as the sensitivity of demand to price, what competitors are doing, and its costs.

■ Whether a firm should spend more on training *depends* on the need for training, the costs of training and the likely benefits.

■ Whether a firm should borrow more money *depends* on what it wants to do with it, the cost of borrowing and the alternative sources of finance.

Once you have analysed your arguments, you can often evaluate by stating that the actual conclusion *depends* on a particular factor (or factors). However, simply writing "it depends on X or Y" is not evaluation – you have to explain why it depends on these things.

So to evaluate, decide:

- Which factor really matters.
- How the firm's actions may differ in the short or long term.
- Why this type of firm (small/large, services/manufacturer, UK-focused/international) might act in a different way from another.
- Why at *this* particular moment or in *these* particular circumstances a firm might behave in a specific way (compared to another situation/different circumstances).

Good and bad practice in exam answers

The two examples below, with examiner's comments, illustrate good and bad practice in answering exam questions.

 Question

The Thatcham Hotel has been doing badly recently. A friend of Farah Sunto, the manager, has suggested she should consult her staff to a greater extent. Discuss the possible benefits of greater consultation in these circumstances.

 Answer: bad practice

Consultation:

- will lead to more ideas
- will mean you find better ways of doing things
- will mean you come up with new ways of doing things
- will motivate
- will keep staff there rather than leaving

Consultation is a good thing and everyone should do it.

Examiner's comment

This answer makes many fundamental mistakes:

a It uses bullet points. Doing this makes it difficult to develop your arguments and examine ideas in depth. It is hard to gain any marks for analysis using bullet points.

b There is no reference to the business situation at all (that is, no application). This answer could be about any firm at any time.

c The last line states that consultation is a "a good thing". The question asks for "discussion", which means the answer should present two sides of an argument and an overview.

d The answer is very definite. It states that consultation always leads to more ideas, always motivates and always means a firm comes up with better ways of doing things. In reality very few things are this definite – especially in business. In Business Studies answers it is better to use words such as "may", "might" or "could" rather than "will". This shows that you appreciate that what you are saying is one possibility among many. For example, the idea that "Consultation will increase motivation" is not necessarily true – some employees may simply think it is an attempt by managers to "steal" their ideas. "Consultation may increase motivation" is true and suggests to the examiner that you appreciate that there are situations when it may not.

Answer: good practice

By consulting with her staff, Farah may be able to get some ideas of how to improve the way the business is run. At the moment it is having problems, so ideas could be useful. The people actually doing the work may have the best thoughts about what is going wrong and what could be done better. With better ideas (for example, about the service in the hotel, the food, the way rooms are cleaned, the booking process and so on) customer satisfaction may increase, which may lead to more revenue and higher profits.

On the other hand, consultation may slow up decision making. This may mean Farah spends lots of time in meetings and discussing things when she could be making decisions. The firm is in trouble at present and may need someone to take action. Asking too many people with lots of different ideas may be interesting but not get anything done in the short term.

Overall, it depends on how the consultation is done and whether it is effective or not. It could lead to more innovation and ways of saving money in the hotel; higher revenue and lower costs could boost profits. However, if too many people are involved in too many things, it may slow up the whole process of management. It may depend on how quickly action must be taken.

Examiner's comment

a   The structure of this answer is good for a "discussion" question: it sets out the case for, the case against and then tries to come to some overall conclusion.

b   It presents a fairly balanced argument, showing that whilst there are benefits from consultation there are also drawbacks and that the overall value "depends".

c   The student attempts to relate the answer to the context of the question – thinking about what might be improved in a hotel and how that would affect the present situation.

d   The student uses the word "may" very effectively, showing an awareness that the actual outcomes in business usually depend on a range of factors.

Marking exam questions – mark scheme

The mark schemes used in the *Marking exam questions* section of each unit follow the AQA approach to marking. All the answers have been marked by identifying the different skills used, and when you mark an answer you should do the same. This will help to familiarise you with the different skills you need to do well in the exam, to recognise what the examiners require and to demonstrate these skills yourself – whichever exam board you are with.

The marked exam questions in each unit are of two types:

■   Questions asking you to **analyse** for a maximum of 8 marks.

■   Questions asking you to **discuss** (**evaluate**) for a maximum of 10 marks.

To mark these questions, use the appropriate mark scheme that follows.

7 mark questions

The questions are marked for Content **C**, Application **AP** and Analysis **AN**.

	Content 2 marks	Application 2 marks	Analysis 3 marks
Level 2	2 marks Candidate shows good understanding of the concept and/or identifies two or more relevant factors.	2 marks Candidate demonstrates good application.	3–2 marks Candidate demonstrates good analysis.
Level 1	1 mark Candidate shows limited understanding of the concept and/or identifies one relevant factor.	1 mark Candidate demonstrates limited application.	1 mark Candidate demonstrates limited analysis.
Level 0	Candidate does not demonstrate understanding of the concept and does not identify any relevant factors.	No application is demonstrated.	No analysis is demonstrated.

10 mark questions

The questions are marked for Content **C**, Application **AP** Analysis **AN** and Evaluation **E**.

	Content 2 marks	Application 2 marks	Analysis 3 marks	Evaluation 3 marks
Level 1	2 marks Candidate offers two or more relevant arguments/shows good understanding	2 marks Candidate applies knowledge effectively to the context	3–2 marks Good analysis of argument	3–2 marks Sound judgement shown in answers and conclusions
Level 2	2 marks Candidate offers single relevant arguments/shows limited understanding	1 mark Candidate attempts to apply knowledge to the context	1 mark Limited analysis of argument	1 mark Some judgement shown in response
Level 0	No relevant context present	0 marks No discernible attempt to apply knowledge to the context	0 marks No analysis demonstrated	0 marks No evaluation present

1.1 Market analysis

Content

- **Market orientation:** when a firm bases its decisions around customer needs and wants. (Also called customer orientation.)
- **Product orientation:** when firms focus on their own operations (for example, improving their products and technology) and hope customers then want to buy their products.
- **Market analysis:** an assessment of market conditions, including market size, market share and market growth.
- **Market size** shows how big a market is. This can be measured by the **volume** (number) of sales (for example, 10 000 units sold) or the **value** of sales (for example, £50m of sales).
- **Market growth** measures the rate at which sales are increasing.
- **Market share** measures one firm's or one brand's sales as a percentage of the total sales in the market.
- **Segmentation:** identifying different groups of similar needs within a market, for example grouping needs by age, lifestyle or geographically.
- **Market research:** gathering, analysing and presenting information relevant to marketing activities, such as consumers' buying behaviour.
- **Primary market research** uses data collected for the first time (also called "field" research). It may be conducted using surveys, interviews and direct observation.
- **Secondary market research** uses information already collected (also called "desk" research). It may be conducted using government publications, newspaper reports and past internal data (for example, sales figures).
- **Quantitative market research** uses large-scale surveys and pre-set questions to provide quantifiable results. For example, it might show the percentage of 16–24 year olds who prefer brand A to brand B. The large sample size makes the findings statistically reliable.
- **Qualitative market research** focuses on consumer attitudes and why consumers behave in a certain way. For example, it might be used to discover what people think of a new advertisement. Qualitative research often uses **focus groups:** a small group of people are interviewed together and asked their opinions on different issues. The small sample size means that these findings are not statistically reliable.
- **Population:** the whole group of people or items that a firm is targeting (for example, all males aged 18–20).
- **Sample:** a selection of a relatively small number of items or people to represent the population as a whole.
- **Random sample:** a sample in which every member of the population has an equal chance of being selected.
- **Quota sample:** a sample in which items or people are selected (non-randomly) to meet given criteria (for example, 50 males aged over 30).
- **Confidence level:** measures the reliability of primary market research. For example, a 95% confidence level means that the findings of the research will be accurate in 19 cases out of 20 (95% of the cases).

Analysis

- Market analysis should help a firm identify which markets are worth entering and which segments to target. Segmentation allows a firm to adjust its marketing mix to meet the needs of customers more fully. Resources can be targeted more effectively and less money is wasted.
- Market research:
  - ☐ provides information that can improve the quality of decision making and reduce the risk of mistakes
  - ☐ can be used to identify opportunities, assess possible courses of action and assess the value of a particular course of action.

  But you need to consider the cost of the research, the time it takes and the most appropriate method to use to find the information you need.

Evaluation

- Market analysis is an essential stage of successful marketing. The better a firm understands a market, the more likely it is to choose the right segments to compete in and to develop an appropriate marketing strategy.
- Competition is likely to be fiercer in a static or declining market, because in this situation a firm can only win more sales at the expense of competitors. In a growing market all firms can sell more.
- A declining market share means that a firm's sales are a smaller proportion of the total. However, sales may still be increasing if the market is growing fast enough.
- To meet customer needs fully, firms can produce a tailor-made item for each customer, but this means sacrificing the benefits of large production runs (for example, economies of scale).
- Market research does not guarantee success. It can improve the chances of getting it right, but success still depends on other factors, such as the product itself, the price and the distribution. Some products succeed with very little research. Others are heavily researched before launching (for example, the children's television programme *Teletubbies*).
- The type of research to use depends on what information is needed. To identify trends such as national income, secondary research may be more sensible. To assess customer reaction to a new product, primary research may be essential.
- The value of market research depends on:
  - ☐ how it is gathered. For example, if a small sample is used, the findings are less likely to be reliable.
  - ☐ the cost of gathering the data
  - ☐ the risk and problems caused by making the wrong decision.
- Market research is more likely to be relevant and up to date if:
  - ☐ the sample size is large,
  - ☐ the research is primary
  - ☐ the sample is selected appropriately.

Examiner's advice

When answering exam questions on market analysis:

- Match the most appropriate method of market research to the type of data required. For example, if a firm sells a product to business customers (such as construction equipment) a questionnaire given to passers-by in the street would not be appropriate.

- For questions about segmentation, think of appropriate ways of segmenting the particular market in the question. For example, the music industry may be segmented according to types of music (classical, pop, rock and roll, drum and bass, garage, etc); the toy industry may be segmented on age (toys targeting the under 5s or over 10s).

- Don't assume that market research is always useful. It may be biased, rushed, based on too small a sample, unnecessary, or take too long. Be willing to question the method *and* the findings.

Market analysis maths

- **Calculating percentage market share**

$$\frac{\text{Brand sales}}{\text{Market sales}} \times 100$$

If the sales of a brand are £25 000 and the total sales in the market are £50 000 the market share is $\frac{£25\,000}{£50\,000} \times 100 = 50\%$

- **Calculating percentage increase**

$$\frac{\text{Change in value}}{\text{Original value}} \times 100$$

Suppose a market is worth £4m and it grows to £5m.

Change in value is +£1m

Percentage increase is $\frac{1}{4} \times 100 = 25\%$

- **Calculating percentages**

Suppose a market has sales of £800m. If the market grows by 5% the new sales can be calculated like this:

The increase in the market size is $\frac{5}{100} \times £800m = £40m$

The new market is worth £800m + £40m = £840m

Worked example 1

A market has grown by 10% and is now worth £440m. What was it worth originally?

As there has been a 10% increase, sales are now 110% compared to their previous level (100% + 10%).

So   110% = £440m

$\quad$ 1% = $\frac{£440m}{110}$ = £4m

$\quad$ 100% = £4m × 100 = £400m

The original sales were £400m.

Worked example 2

A market is worth £300 000. A firm has a market share of 15%. What is the value of the firm's share?

$\frac{15}{100} \times £300\,000 = £45\,000$

1.1 Market analysis

Practice questions

Maths questions

1 The total number of products sold in a market is 25 000. The average price per unit is £6. What is the market size in £?

2 A product's sales are £120 000. Total market sales are £600 000. What is the product's market share?

3 A market was worth £300 000. It is now worth £400 000. How much has the market grown?

4 A market is worth £400 000. It grows by 5% each year. How big is the market after
   a 1 year
   b 2 years?

5 A firm has a market share of 20% of a market worth £200 000. The market grows by 50% but the firm's sales stay constant. What is the firm's new market share?

Diagram questions

1 Look at the left-hand diagram, below.
   Brand A has sales of £160m.
   a What is the value of the market as a whole?
   Brand C has 62% of the market.
   b What is the market share of brand B?
   c What is the value of sales of brand B?
   Look at the right-hand diagram. Suppose that the market has doubled in size but the value of sales of Brand A have remained the same.
   d Shade in the new market share for Brand A.

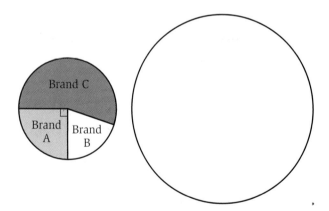

2 a What is the percentage market growth from year 1 to year 2 in the market shown opposite?

   b Sales are expected to grow by 25% in year 3.
   Draw in a bar to show this.

   c A firm is proposing to enter this market in year 3.
   It predicts that it will gain a 5% market share. What will its forecasted sales be?

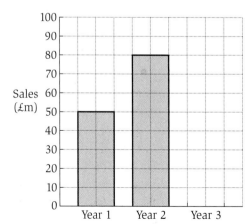

Quick questions

1 A 95% confidence level means that 95% of a firm's products will be successful. True or false?

2 Unscramble these letters to find two words that describe how a market can be divided into groups of similar needs and wants.
ETKMAR ONETIGENSMTA

3 The government often publishes information about the economy, such as national income data. If a firm makes use of this it is using *primary/secondary/qualitative* data. Choose the correct option.

4 The findings of a survey are more likely to be reliable if the sample size is large. True or false?

5 Using primary market research is likely to be *quicker/slower* and *more expensive/cheaper* than using secondary market research.
Choose the correct options.

6 With a quota sample, all members of the population have an equal chance of selection. True or false?

7 A researcher stands on the street corner and asks 200 passers-by what they think of a recent government proposal. This is an example of a *random/quota/secondary* sample.
Choose the correct option.

8 A company used a focus group of 10 people to select a name for a new film. The group preferred the name *Love Dreams* to *Soppy Stories*. This is an example of *secondary/qualitative/quantitative* research.
Choose the correct option.

9 To research what customers think of a new brand name, you are more likely to use *primary/secondary* research.
Choose the correct option. Explain your answer.

10 Competition between firms is likely to be fiercer in a *growing/declining* market.
Choose the correct option. Explain your answer.

11 State the equation you would use to calculate *Coca-Cola's* market share of the UK soft drinks market.

12 A firm that has a low market share in one market may have higher sales than a firm with a higher market share in another market.
Explain why.

13 An increase in sales does not always increase profits.
Explain why.

14 State two ways of measuring the size of a market.

15 If a market is well established, this makes it more likely that in future it will grow at a *slow/fast* rate.
Choose the correct option. Explain your answer.

What did you score?
Now check your answers, giving yourself one mark for each one correct.
If you scored:

12–15 **Congratulations! You clearly know these topics well. Now move on to the next section.**

8–11 **This is quite a good score. It shows that you know some sections of these topics. However, there are some areas you need to revise. Why not look over the material again before moving on to the next section?**

Less than 8 **This is less than half marks. You obviously need to revise these topics again.**

Marking exam answers

Question

Marisa Shahrir owns a restaurant in Bristol. She is trying to decide whether to open a second restaurant in the area. Analyse two possible benefits to Marisa of using market research to help her make the decision. **(7 marks)**

Marked answer

Market research may help Marisa to identify the most appropriate part of the city in which to open, for example it may identify where there is a lot of competition. **C** It may also help her decide what sort of restaurant to open, **C** for example the menu, the prices and the way it should it position and promote itself compared to other restaurants in the area. **AP** For example, if there are several French restaurants nearby she might want to open one which offers different food so she can differentiate her business, therefore attracting more customers, which may lead to higher profits. **AN**

By understanding the market better, Marisa could focus her marketing activities and not waste resources. **C** For example, she could identify the type of customer she wants, where they live and where to advertise to attract them, such as in the local papers or on the local radio. **AP** This type of advertising would work if most of her customers were local (rather than people travelling a long distance to eat) and therefore she could save money by not wasting it on inappropriate advertising. **AN**

> ### Examiner's comment
> The answer is good in that it identifies, applies and analyses two relevant benefits effectively (for example, what to offer and where to advertise). The candidate tries to keep the answer in context by referring to the menu and where customers are likely to come from (gaining application marks).
> Although the candidate identifies three benefits there is no extra credit for this.
> **Mark: Content: 2/2 Application: 2/2 Analysis: 3/3 Total: 7/7**

Your chance to mark

Mark the answer to this question, using the marking scheme on page xvii.

Question

After working for five years in magazine publishing, Sam Ahmed is eager to start up his own business. Before launching a new magazine he wants to undertake market research to identify what market segments exist. Discuss two possible benefits to Sam of identifying segments within the highly competitive magazine market. **(10 marks)**

Student answer

Segmentation involves identifying groups of similar needs in a market. If Sam uses market research to identify segments, he can choose which one or ones to target and change his products to meet their needs more precisely. In this case he may include particular features they like and get journalists to write articles that his target group would like to read. For example, young men may want something about music; retired people may want something about gardening.

By providing something people really want, Sam should be able to produce a magazine that is better than the competitors and therefore attract more readers. This way he should have better customer satisfaction and loyalty and be able to earn more profits. If the market is competitive it is particularly important to target what you offer very closely so that you don't lose customers to someone else.

Mark: Content: _ /2 Application: _ /2 Analysis: _ /3 Evaluation: _ /3 Total: _ /10

Now look at page 109 to compare your comments and marks with the examiner's.

1.2 Marketing strategy

Content

- **Marketing objective:** a quantifiable marketing target, for example to increase sales by 20% over two years.
- **Marketing strategy:** a long-term plan to achieve the marketing objective. For example, a firm's decision to focus its marketing efforts on overseas markets rather than the domestic market, in order to boost sales.
- **Marketing tactics:** short-term plans to implement the marketing strategy. For example, a firm's decision to cut the price for a few weeks as part of a promotional offer.
- The **product life cycle** shows how the sales of a product change over time.

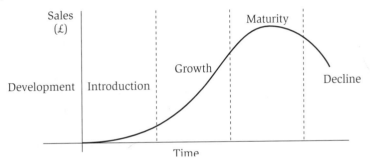

- **Determinism:** when a manager's beliefs about what might happen actually cause this event to occur. For example, if a manager thinks sales will fall she may spend less on promotion, which could then *cause* sales to decline.
- **Extension strategy:** an attempt to maintain the sales of a product and prevent the decline stage of the product life cycle.
- **Product portfolio analysis:** when a firm examines the position of all of its products in the market.
- **Boston Matrix:** a method of product portfolio analysis that assesses products' positions in terms of market share and market growth. Also called the Boston Box. Each circle represents a product. The area of the circle represents its turnover (the larger the circle, the higher the turnover).

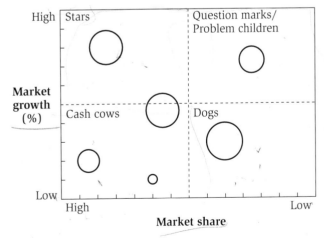

- ☐ A **cash cow** is a product that has a large market share in a slow growing market.
- ☐ A **dog** is a product that has a low market share in a slow growing market.
- ☐ A **star** is a product that has a high market share in a fast growing market.
- ☐ A **question mark** is a product that has a low market share in a fast growing market. (Also called a **problem child**.)

- **Niche marketing:** a strategy that focuses on a specific segment of the market (usually a small segment).
- **Mass marketing:** a strategy aimed at the majority of consumers in the market.
- **Capacity utilisation:** the amount a firm is producing relative to the maximum amount it could be producing given its resources. It is measured as a percentage; for example 80% capacity utilisation means the firm's output is 80% of its maximum capacity.
- **Unique Selling Point (USP):** a feature of a product that differentiates it from its competitors; for example, a shop stays open later than its rivals.
- **Adding value:** increasing the perceived benefits of a product in the eyes of the customer, so that the difference between what a customer will pay and production costs increases. For example, it may only cost shops a little to deliver items direct to customers' homes, but they may be able to charge quite a lot for this additional service.

Analysis

- The marketing objective should always be linked to the corporate objective.
- Setting a marketing objective provides a direction for the firm's marketing activities. This enables marketing activities to be coordinated more easily.
- A niche marketing strategy may be a means of competing without fighting head on with the larger producers.
- The product life cycle only looks at one product. However, most firms have many products and they may want an overview of all their products at once.
- Cash flow is likely to be negative in the build up to the product launch and in the early stages of the product's life, due to investment in development and promotion. Cash flow is only likely to become positive when sales are growing significantly.
- To prevent the decline stage of the product life cycle, a firm may use an extension strategy, for example cutting price, increasing promotion or trying to find new uses for the product. Alternatively a firm may develop a new model or even a completely new product to take over from the old one. As the sales of the old product decline, sales of the new one may be increasing.
- Capacity utilisation is likely to be low when a product is first launched, because sales are low. This means that the unit cost is likely to be high. As sales increase, capacity utilisation increases. This means that the fixed costs can be spread over more units, reducing the unit cost.
- In the early stages of the life cycle, the high initial unit costs may result in low profits or even losses.
- Product portfolio analysis gives a firm an overview of its business and enables it to plan what to do with different products. For example, it may stop producing 'dog' products and invest more in 'star' products.
- A USP can help a firm to add value. This might enable it to charge a higher price than its competitors.
- There can be many different types of marketing objective. Typically a firm will want to increase sales but this is not always the case. For example, if capacity is limited a firm might want to boost sales of some products (the more profitable ones) at the expense of others. In a seasonal business the aim might be to achieve a steadier pattern of sales.
- A mass marketing strategy requires high volumes of production. This is likely to require a high level of initial investment (for example, in production lines).

- As sales increase in the growth phases of the product life cycle, many of the marketing costs (for example, promotional costs) can be spread over more units. Initially the marketing costs per unit are likely to be high because not many units are being sold and the firm may have to spend heavily to raise awareness of the product.

- The marketing of a product is likely to change at different stages of the product life cycle. In the early stages, promotion may be aimed at increasing awareness (letting customers know that it exists and telling them what it does). Later the emphasis may be more focused on explaining why the product is better than similar products that have since been launched by competitors. The price may initially be set quite high, especially if the product has a unique selling point, but may have to be decreased over time as competitors enter the market. At first distribution may be limited because distributors are unwilling to take a risk with a new product. If the product begins to succeed, getting wider distribution should be easier.

Evaluation　　　　　　　　　　　　　　　　　　　　　　**E**

- The success of a marketing plan depends on whether an appropriate strategy is chosen. If a firm decides to compete in a market which then declines, it is less likely to succeed.

- Niche marketing may be risky because the market is relatively small and a firm may be very dependent on a few customers. If these customers stop buying, the fall in the firm's sales may be significant.

- Mass marketing can be expensive for a firm to undertake, since it may require heavy investment in production facilities. It is only likely to be successful if demand is high and fairly standardised (that is, if customers want all the products to be similar).

- A firm may have a USP but others may imitate it. The firm should consider whether it can protect its USP, for example by taking out a patent.

- Product portfolio analysis and the product life cycle are models used to help analyse the business situation. They do not guarantee success – this depends on how they are used, whether the right decisions are then taken and whether these are implemented correctly.

- The length of the product life cycle will depend on
  - ☐ the type of product (for example, pop stars often have a limited appeal and films are usually popular for a few months only, whereas a successful model of car may last a couple of years)
  - ☐ the effectiveness of the marketing
  - ☐ the ease with which the product can be imitated or further developed.

  Improvements in technology have tended to shorten product life cycles, as "new, improved" products are launched regularly. The mobile phone market shows how a particular model may only last a few months due to technological change.

- It is possible to distinguish between the life cycle of the product category (for example, cars) and the life cycle of a particular product model or brand (for example the Ford *Mondeo*). The life cycle of a particular brand is usually much shorter than that of the product category as a whole. Having said this some brands, such as *Kellogg's* Cornflakes, Pears soap, *Mars* bars have been around for many years.

1.2 Marketing strategy

Marketing strategy maths

■ **Calculating capacity utilisation**

$$\text{Capacity utilisation} = \frac{\text{Existing output}}{\text{Maximum possible output}} \times 100$$

For example, if the present output is 300 units and the maximum possible output is 600 units:

$$\text{Capacity utilisation} = \frac{300}{600} \times 100 = 50\%$$

Practice questions

Maths questions

1 Xejo plc has the capacity to produce 80 000 units a week. At present it is operating at 40% capacity utilisation.
How many units is it currently producing each week?

2 Remo has spent £2.6m launching and promoting its latest film *Dinosaur* this year. Other spending on the film has amounted to £2.8m. So far 2.2m people have seen the film at the cinema; on average the film company receives £3 per viewer. What is the company's current cash flow position for this film?

3 A firm is able to produce 2000 units a week. At present it is producing 400. What is its capacity utilisation?

4 Brenda Hanji is reviewing the sales of one of her company's products.

	£
Sales this year	25 500
Sales last year	25 000
Sales two years ago	20 000
Sales three years ago	12 000

Where do you think this product is in its life cycle? Explain your answer.

Diagram questions

1 Write these labels in the correct sections of the Boston Matrix:
Dog
Cash cow
Star
Question mark

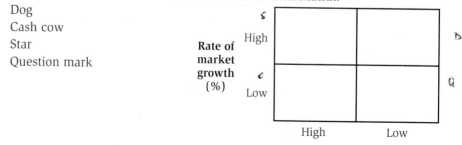

2 Four stages of the product life cycle are:
decline
maturity
growth
introduction

  a Label these stages on the diagram below.

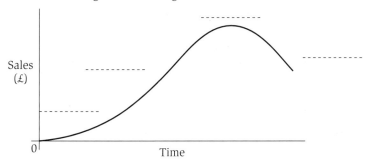

  b Identify where the following products are in the product life cycle:
typewriters
Mars bars
videophones
DVDs

  c On the diagram in part **a**, draw:
A line to show the cash flow at different stages of the life cycle.
A line to show the effects of an extension strategy on sales.

  d On the diagram below, draw a line to show a new product (Product B) being launched to take over sales from this one.

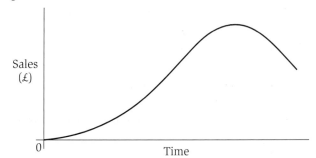

Quick questions

1 "To increase sales by 20% over two years."
This is an example of a marketing *objective/strategy/tactic/life cycle*. Choose the correct option.

2 A firm decides to focus its efforts on a small segment of the market, rather than competing in the mainstream market. This is known as a marketing *portfolio/strategy/objective/examination*.
Choose the correct option.

3 The product life cycle shows what happens to the sales of a product in relation to .... (*Hint:* Think of the labels on the axes!)

4 When a firm increases the benefits offered to customers relative to the costs of providing the good, this is known as a........... v..........

5 The axes of the Boston Matrix show sales and time. True or false?

6   When sales are increasing at a faster rate each period, this is known as the
    .... stage of the product life cycle.

7   In the Boston Matrix model a cash cow has a *high/low* market share and sells in
    a *fast/slow* growing market.
    Choose the correct options.

8   A product category in the Boston Matrix model that has a low market share but
    sells in a fast growing market: NQIOESUT RKAM. Unscramble the letters.

9   In the Boston Matrix model a dog product has a *high/low* market share and sells
    in a *fast/slow* growing market.
    Choose the correct options.

10 A niche market tends to have lower total sales than a mass market. True or false?

11 In the early stages of the product life cycle the capacity utilisation is likely to be
    high/low.
    Choose the correct option. Explain your answer.

12 When a firm tries to maintain the sales of a product and prevent the decline
    stage of the life cycle occurring, this is known as an
    extenuating/declension/extension/portfolio strategy.
    Choose the correct option.

13 When a firm examines the market position of all of its products this is known as
    RUPCTOD TFPIOOLRO LSIYASNA. Unscramble the letters.

14 Some people argue that if you believe that sales of a product are about to
    decline, you are less likely to make the effort to keep them high so they
    probably will fall. This idea that if you believe something is going to happen
    this may make it happen is known as ....

15 A star product has *high/low* market share and sells in a *fast/slow* growing market.
    Choose the correct options.

What did you score?
Now check your answers, giving yourself one mark for each one correct.
If you scored:

12–15   **Congratulations! You clearly know these topics well. Now move on
            to the next section.**

8–11   **This is quite a good score. It shows that you know some sections of
            these topics. However, there are some areas you need to revise.
            Why not look over the material again before moving on to the next
            section?**

Less than 8 **This is less than half marks. You obviously need to revise these
            topics again.**

Marking exam questions

Question
Mike Fulson runs a busy shop in North Oxford that makes and sells sandwiches. His
customers are mainly local business people. Discuss ways in which Mike could add
value to the service he provides.   **(10 marks)**

Marked answer
Adding value involves increasing the perceived benefits to the customer. **C** In this
case this could be allowing business people to order in advance by phone. This would
mean they do not have to queue when they want lunch and therefore they can get on
with their own work for longer. **AP** They may be willing to pay more for sandwiches
from Mike to save time because of the extra benefit this provides. **AN**

Mike could also deliver to the places where people work. **C** This also saves the customer time and their companies may be willing to pay because it gets more work out of people and so even if they pay more for the sandwiches they might actually save money overall. **AP** **AN**

The way in which Mike adds value for his customers depends on what customers actually want. After all, whether something provides "value" depends on the customers' perception. For example, business people might prefer to have somewhere to sit and eat their sandwiches in Mike's shop because this gives them a break from the office and a chance for a rest. In this case he may want to make more space in the shop to sit. **E** **AP**

Examiner's comment

This is a very strong answer indeed. The candidate clearly shows an understanding of the concept and relates it to the actual product and scenario. The question asks you to "discuss" so a good answer will weigh up the arguments or show judgement in some form. In this case the candidate evaluates by highlighting that how you add value depends on your customers and what they want – for example your customers may want to stay for longer at work or they may want an excuse to get out the office.

Mark: Content: 2/2 Application: 2/2 Analysis: 3/3 Evaluation: 3/3 Total: 10/10

Your chance to mark
Mark the answer to this question, using the marking scheme on page xvii.

Question
Jes Diamond has been a producer for big record companies such as EMI for ten years. He has decided to set up his own record label. This will involve signing bands, recording their music and marketing their CDs. Jes believes that the best strategy is to focus on a niche he has identified in the market for Asian drum and bass. This is the music he likes. Discuss the possible advantages and disadvantages to Jes of choosing a niche marketing strategy for his new business. **(10 marks)**

Student answer
Jes might want to target a niche because this is a small part of the market. This means that the big firms may not be interested in his business. A niche may be a specialist business which is quite exclusive and so you can charge a lot for the work you do because it is different from the competition. People may be prepared to pay because it is so special and unique. However a niche market may not be very big and so it may not be possible to make lots of profits in it compared to a mass market. Also to be niche may mean you have to tailor make your services to your clients so you have to be flexible which can be difficult and you may not have the skills. Also a niche market is vulnerable to changes in demand – if only a few customers stop buying this can have a big effect on the overall sales, because the market is so small.

Mark: Content: _/2 Application: _/2 Analysis: _/3 Evaluation: _/3 Total: _/10

Now look at page 110 to compare your comments and marks with the examiner's.

1.3 Marketing planning

Content

- **Marketing mix:** all the different elements that combine to influence a customer's decision to purchase an item, for example the price, the way it is promoted, the product itself and the way it is distributed. The marketing mix is often described as the 4Ps: Price, Product, Place (distribution) and Promotion.
- **Price skimming:** a pricing strategy where a high initial price is charged when a product is launched.
- **Price taker:** a firm that follows the price set by others in the market.
- **Predatory pricing:** a pricing strategy where a firm sets a low price to undercut the competitors and force them out of the market.
- **Penetration pricing:** a pricing strategy where a firm sets a low initial price for a product entering the market, in an attempt to gain market share.
- **Loss leader:** the price of an item is set at a low level to entice customers into the shop to buy other products.
- **Cost-plus pricing:** a pricing technique where a percentage or amount of profit is added to the unit costs.
- **Contribution pricing:** a pricing technique where the price is set to exceed the variable costs per unit, so that there is a contribution per unit (see page 25) to fixed costs.
- **Price discrimination:** different prices are set for the same product or service; for example, a taxi charging different rates according to the time of day.
- **Psychological pricing:** setting the price based on the expectations of the target customer group. For example, a price of £9.99 rather than £10 may make customers buy because they think it is a bargain; or a high price may convince customers that the service is of high quality.
- **Above the line promotion:** methods of promotion that use the main advertising media, for example television and print advertising.
- **Below the line promotion:** methods of promotion that do not use the main advertising media (are not above the line); for example, sales promotions, competitions and offers, personal selling.
- **Distribution channel:** describes how the ownership of a product or service moves from the manufacturer to the final customer, for example from manufacturer to wholesaler to retailer.
- **Distribution targets:** objectives set for distribution, for example to increase distribution through certain types of outlet or in certain regions.

Analysis

- A firm's marketing planning must relate to the marketing strategy. For example, if a firm is trying to win customers by differentiating itself, this may require a product with very distinctive features, which may in turn require a particular approach to promotion and a high price. If the strategy is to compete with a low price, this may involve a more basic product.
- The marketing mix must be integrated to work effectively – the price must fit with the promotion and so on. For example, a heavily branded, well promoted product distributed through exclusive shops is likely to have a high price.
- Marketing activities must be linked to other areas of the business. For example, whether a firm can offer low prices depends on its costs.

Evaluation

- The role of price depends on how sensitive demand is to price. This is measured by the **price elasticity of demand** (see page 19). Some products are less sensitive to price than others (for example, diamonds are less price sensitive than washing machines).
- The right method of promotion depends on the type of product. Industrial products such as production equipment tend to be sold via personal selling. Television advertising for this sort of product is unlikely.
- The right method of promotion also depends on the audience, the cost and the effectiveness of different media.
- The nature of the product is a key element of its success. Consider its features, its reliability, its ease of repair and its after-sales service.
- The most effective distribution channel depends on the type of product. An exclusive item may be distributed to certain closely controlled outlets. Other items such as soft drinks need to be distributed to a wide range of outlets. Some firms have been successful by finding new ways to distribute their products, for example Direct Line insurance (by telephone); First Direct (the first telephone banking service); Dell (direct sales by telephone or internet).
- The relative importance of the different elements of the marketing mix depends on the product. For example, for a Christmas gift or for perfume, the packaging is likely to be very important; when selling a bulldozer the packaging may be less significant.
- The relative importance of the elements of the marketing mix also depends on the customer. For a customer without much money, the price is very important.
- The overall success of a business depends heavily on the effectiveness of its marketing (otherwise people won't know that the product exists or be prepared to buy it). But it also depends on the other business functions. For example, it needs production to make the product and human resource management to provide the right number of employees with the right skills.

Examiner's advice

When answering exam questions on market analysis:

- The marketing mix is meant to be a model that can help you analyse the way a good or service is marketed. In reality it often seems to act as a constraint and sometimes seems to prevent students from thinking intelligently! Don't just go through the mix listing each element and producing a standard textbook answer, such as:
  "The price is very important. It must be just right – it cannot be too high or no one buys. Advertising is important – you can advertise on television or radio. Distribution – the product must be distributed to the right places."
  Remember to think carefully about the specific product you have been asked about and which elements of the marketing mix really matter for *this* type of good or service. For example, advertising may be very important for selling chocolate but not for selling tractors.
- When you are asked about marketing or the marketing mix, be careful not to write only about advertising. This is only one form of promotion and is often a small part of the overall marketing mix.

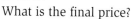
Marketing planning maths

- **Calculating percentage mark up and final price**
  The cost per unit is £20. There is a cost-plus pricing policy with a mark up of 10%.
  What is the final price?

  $$10\% \text{ of } £20 = \frac{10}{100} \times £20 = £2$$

  So final selling price is £20 + £2 = £22

Practice questions

Maths questions

1. A retailer buys in products and adds on 25% to set the final price. If the retailer buys the products for £4, what will it sell them for?

2. A firm produces 300 units. Its total costs are £600. The firm's policy is to add 10% to its unit costs to set the price.
   What price will it charge for the product?

3. Marcham Ltd produces greetings cards. Marcham's distribution target is to have its cards in 40% of the possible outlets in the local area by the end of the year. The managers estimate that there are 2000 outlets in the surrounding area where Marcham could sell its cards. At present Marcham's cards are in 350 of these outlets.
   How many more outlets must Marcham's cards sell in to achieve the distribution target?

Diagram questions

1. On the diagram, sketch lines to illustrate:
   a the price of a product over time under a price skimming policy.
   b the price of a product over time under a penetration pricing policy.

   Price

   Time

2. Write these three stages of marketing in the boxes in the correct order.
   ☐ Marketing strategy
   ☐ Marketing planning
   ☐ Marketing objectives
   Give an example of each.

   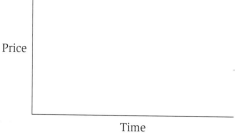

Quick questions

1 A price skimming strategy is more likely if a product has a USP. True or false?

2 Setting a low initial price when a product is launched to gain market share is known as *price skimming/contribution pricing/penetration pricing/price discrimination*.
   Choose the correct option.

3 Television advertising is an example of below the line promotion.
   True or false?

4 To make a profit the price must be higher than *the demand/the cost per unit/the sales/the revenue*.
   Choose the correct option.

5 John runs a petrol station. To set his prices he looks at the prices being charged by a garage further up the road and matches them. John is a price ....

6 Julie buys clothes from a factory in the Far East for £40 per garment on average. She adds on 50%. What is her average selling price?
   This method is known as ....-........... pricing.

7 Advertising, special offers, competitions and public relations are all examples of ORPNMOOIT.
   Unscramble the letters.

8 Personal selling is an example of above the line promotion.
   True or false?

9 Stars night club charges different entry prices on different days, according to demand. Charging different prices for the same service is known as ....
   ....

10 Fantasmo Cola wants its products sold in 20% of newsagents in the UK by 2005. This is known as a d................... t..............

11 To achieve a market share of 25% is a *marketing objective/marketing strategy/marketing analysis*.
   Choose the correct option.

12 Price skimming is most likely when there are *few/many* competitors.
   Choose the correct option. Explain your answer.

13 When Music Box opened up near the Sounds record shop, Sounds slashed all its prices to drive the new entrant out of business. This is called .... pricing.

14 A firm is most likely to use a price penetration strategy to enter a market when there are major cost advantages from producing on a *small/large* scale.
   Choose the correct option. Explain your answer.

15 Promotional offers are an example of below the line promotion.
   True or false?

What did you score?
Now check your answers, giving yourself one mark for each one correct.
If you scored:

12–15   **Congratulations! You clearly know these topics well. Now move on to the next section.**

8–11   **This is quite a good score. It shows that you know some sections of these topics. However, there are some areas you need to revise. Why not look over the material again before moving on to the next section?**

Less than 8   **This is less than half marks. You obviously need to revise these topics again.**

Marking exam answers

Question

Ando Ltd has just launched a new computer game and has adopted a price skimming strategy. Analyse *two* possible reasons why the firm might have adopted this type of pricing strategy.

(7 marks)

Marked answer

A price skimming strategy means that a high price is set when a product is introduced into the market. **C** A firm may maintain a high price if it knows that demand for the product will still be high. This may occur when the product is innovative or has a USP or there are few substitutes, because people won't want to or be able to switch and therefore a high price will not damage demand too much. **AN** If a product is seen as exclusive then the high price might fit with its image. **C** A high price might also be possible in a protected market. **C**

> ## Examiner's comment
> The student clearly understands price skimming and in the first part of the answer makes a reasonable attempt to develop the argument. After this the candidate simply presents a couple of new ideas without developing these points.
>
> The weakness of this answer is that it does not relate the analysis to the context of a computer game – it could be an answer about anything. A stronger answer would have referred to particular features of the game (for example, special effects) or the value of a strong brand name (for example, Lara Croft).
>
> **Mark: Content: 2/2   Application: 0/2   Analysis: 2/3   Total: 4/7**

Your chance to mark

Mark the answer to this question, using the marking scheme on page xvii.

Question

Estelle Dimka has just finished at university and has set up a shop in Oxford selling clothes. She has used up nearly all of her savings to start up the business and believes that she will soon be making a profit. The city is home to quite a lot of students and young people and in the summer many tourists visit as well. She is targeting the 18–24 age group, stocking clothes not found in more mainstream stores.

Discuss the ways in which Estelle might promote her new business. **(10 marks)**

Student answer

Estelle could promote the business by advertising. This would probably be local advertising because many of her customers live locally. She may try putting notices up at the colleges and universities to let the students know about her shop. She shouldn't try local radio unless she can find a station this age group listens to. She may also use the shop itself to attract attention – something which will make people come in, for example a good window display or a "just open" offer.

Estelle does not have a lot of money and so any promotion she does will have to be relatively cheap. She also has a problem in that Oxford has a lot of tourists and as these people are passing through they may be difficult to reach. Also the students are only there at certain times of the year, so the timing of the promotion may be important.

Mark: Content: _/2 Application: _/2 Analysis: _/3 Evaluation: _/3 Total: _/10

Now look at page 110 to compare your comments and marks with the examiner's.

1.4 Elasticity of demand

Content

- **Demand:** measures the quantity that customers are willing and able to purchase at different prices (assuming other factors such as income, advertising and competitors' prices stay the same).
- **Price elasticity of demand:** measures how responsive demand is to changes in price.

  Price elasticity = $\dfrac{\text{Percentage change in quantity demanded}}{\text{Percentage change in price}}$
- **Income elasticity of demand:** measures how responsive demand is to changes in customer income.

  Income elasticity = $\dfrac{\text{Percentage change in quantity demanded}}{\text{Percentage change in income}}$

Analysis

- The level of demand for a product depends on factors such the price, income levels, the availability of alternatives and the firm's promotion strategy.
- The price elasticity of demand usually has a negative answer, because an **increase** in price (+) usually **reduces** the quantity demanded (−) and vice versa. Because they move in opposite directions the answer is negative.
- The income elasticity of demand usually has a positive answer because an **increase** in income (+) usually **increases** the quantity demanded (+) and vice versa. Because they move in the same direction the answer is positive. However, for some goods (known as inferior goods) an increase in income (+) will reduce sales (−), so the income elasticity for these items is negative.
- To assess the **value** of the elasticity, ignore the sign. For example −2 and +2 both have the value 2.
- Demand is price elastic if the price elasticity has value more than 1 (if the percentage change in quantity demanded is *bigger* than the percentage change in price).
- Demand is price inelastic if the price elasticity has value less than 1 (if the percentage change in the quantity demanded is *less* than the percentage change in price).
- Demand is income elastic if the income elasticity has value more than 1 (if the percentage change in the quantity demanded is *bigger* than the percentage change in income).
- Demand is income inelastic if the income elasticity has value less than 1 (if the percentage change in the quantity demanded is *less* than the percentage change in income).
- The price elasticity shows how much the demand changes with changes in price. For example, a price elasticity value of –2 means that a percentage change in price will lead to a change in quantity demanded that is twice as big. For example, a 10% fall in price will increase sales by 20%.
- The income elasticity shows how much the quantity demanded changes as customer income changes. For example, an income elasticity value of 0.5 means that a percentage change in income will lead to a change in the quantity demanded that is half as big. For example, a 10% fall in income will decrease sales by 5%.

- If demand is price elastic, a cut in price will increase revenue (although the price is lower, the higher sales more than compensate for this). The effect on profits depends on what happens to costs when more units are sold.
- If demand is price inelastic, a cut in price will reduce revenue (the increase in sales is not enough to compensate for the lower price). An increase in price will increase revenue.
- The demand for a product is likely to be price inelastic if the product has few substitutes, is heavily branded or has a Unique Selling Point (USP).
- Price elasticity can help a firm to determine:
  - **a** whether or not to increase or decrease the price
  - **b** the impact of a price change on sales (which has implications for production and staffing).
- Income elasticity can help a firm to determine:
  - **a** what might happen to its sales if the economy or region grows or declines
  - **b** whether it has the right mix of products for the present and future economic climate (for example, should it introduce a different type of product?).

Evaluation

- The usefulness of the concept of elasticity depends on how the values have been calculated. For example, if the price elasticity is based on past data it may not be relevant.
- Remember that the values may change over time.
- The price elasticity of demand may be used to predict the impact on quantity demanded if price alone changes. However, it is likely that many other factors are changing as well, such as the firm's advertising or the state of the economy. This may reduce the value of the concept.
- Income elasticity of demand helps a firm predict the impact on quantity demanded if income alone changes. However, many other things may also be changing (for example, competitors' prices and promotional campaigns). This may reduce the value of the concept.

Examiner's advice

When answering exam questions on elasticity of demand:

- Students often forget that the equations for elasticity compare percentage changes rather than absolute numbers.
- Students often state the equations the wrong way around (with the quantity demanded on the bottom rather than the top line of the equation).
- In elasticity calculations, students often multiply the answer by 100 and state it as a percentage. Remember that price and income elasticities are numbers, not percentages.
- Students often confuse price elasticity and income elasticity and use the two interchangeably. One shows what happens to the quantity demanded when price changes. The other shows what happens to the quantity demanded when income changes. They are not the same.
- Make sure that you use the terms precisely. Price inelastic means that a percentage price change leads to a *smaller* percentage change in demand. It does not mean that you can charge what you like without affecting demand at all!

Elasticity of demand maths

 ■ **Calculating percentage change**

$$\frac{\text{Change in value}}{\text{Original value}} \times 100$$

Worked example 1

a A price rises from £5 to £6. What is the percentage increase?

Change in value is £6 − £5 = £1

Using the formula:

Percentage change $= \dfrac{1}{5} \times 100 = 20\%$

b A price falls from £10 to £6. What is the percentage decrease?

Percentage change $= \dfrac{-4}{10} \times 100 = -40\%$

Worked example 2

The price elasticity of demand is −2.

a What is the effect on sales of a 10% increase in price?

The price elasticity shows how much the quantity demanded changes relative to a price change. The value is −2, which means the quantity demanded changes twice as much (because the value is 2) and in the opposite direction (because the value is negative).

So a 10% price increase leads to a 2 × 10 = 20% decrease in quantity demanded.

b What is the effect on sales of a 20% decrease in price?

This would lead to a 2 × 20% = 40% increase in quantity demanded.

Worked example 3

The income elasticity of demand is +0.5.

a What is the effect on sales of a 10% increase in income?

The income elasticity shows how much the quantity demanded changes relative to an income change. If the value is +0.5, this means the quantity demanded changes half as much (because the value is 0.5) and in the same direction (because the value is positive).

So a 10% income increase leads to a 0.5 × 10 = 5% increase in quantity demanded.

b What is the effect on sales of a 20% decrease in income?

This would lead to a 0.5 × 20% = 10% decrease in quantity demanded.

Worked example 4

The income elasticity of demand is −3.

a What is the effect on sales of a 10% increase in income?

The income elasticity shows how much the quantity demanded changes relative to an income change. If the value is −3 this means the quantity demanded changes three times as much (because the value is 3) and in a different direction (because the value is negative).

So a 10% income increase leads to a 3 × 10 = 30% decrease in quantity demanded.

b What is the effect on sales of a 20% decrease in income?

This would lead to a 3 × 20% = 60% increase in quantity demanded.

Practice questions

Maths questions

1 The price of a product is cut from £5 to £4.
   Sales increase from 300 units to 400 units.
   a What is the percentage change in the quantity demanded?
   b What is the percentage change in price?
   c What is the price elasticity of demand?
   d Is the demand price elastic or price inelastic? Explain your answer.
   e What was the old revenue? (*Hint:* Revenue = Price × Quantity of sales)
   f What is the new revenue?
   g What do your answers suggest about the relationship between price cuts, elasticity and revenue?

2 In the country of Atlantica, the average annual income has increased from £20 000 to £22 000. The number of swimming pools sold per year has increased from 50 000 to 60 000. The cost of a swimming pool is £15 000.
   a Calculate the percentage change in the quantity demanded.
   b Calculate the percentage change in income.
   c Calculate the income elasticity of demand.
   Is this income elastic or inelastic? Explain your answer.
   d What was the old revenue?
   e What is the new revenue?

3 The price elasticity of demand for a product is −2. If you cut the price by 10%, what do you expect to happen to sales? Explain your answer.

4 The income elasticity of demand for a product is +0.5. If income increases by 10%, what do you expect to happen to sales? Explain your answer.

Diagram questions

1 Complete the table:

Change in quantity demanded (units)	Change in price (£)	% change in quantity demanded	% change in price	Price elasticity of demand	Price elastic or inelastic
100 to 150	10 to 9	$+\frac{50}{100} \times 100$ $= +50\%$	$-\frac{1}{10} \times 100$ $= -10\%$	$+\frac{50}{-10} = -5$	Elastic
40 to 50	5 to 3				
20 to	8 to 4	$+10\%$			
200 to 160	50 to		$+10\%$	-2	

2 Complete the table:

Change in quantity demanded (units)	Change in price (£)	Price elasticity	Elastic or inelastic	Old revenue	New revenue	Comment?
400 to 480 $= \frac{80}{400} \times 100$ $= +20\%$	£10 to £9 $= -\frac{1}{10} \times 100$ $= -10\%$	$+\frac{20}{-10} = -2$	Elastic	400 × £10 $= £4000$	480 × £9 $= £4320$	Price elastic; lowering price increases revenue
400 to 420	£10 to £8					
400 to 390	£10 to £15					

Quick questions

1 The relationship between a change in quantity demanded and a change in price is measured by the .... elasticity of demand.

2 The relationship between a change in the quantity demanded and a change in income is measured by the .... elasticity of demand.

3 If a good is price elastic, the value of the price elasticity (ignoring the sign) is .... than 1.

4 If a good is price inelastic, the value of the price elasticity (ignoring the sign) is .... than 1.

5 If a good is price inelastic, then a change in price does not affect the quantity demanded at all. True or false?

6 If a good is income elastic, then a change in price brings about a bigger change in demand. True or false?

7 A price falls from £10 to £9.
What is the percentage change?

8 A price increases from £9 to £10.
What is the percentage change?

9 A 10% increase in income leads to a 20% increase in sales.
What is the income elasticity of demand?

10 A 50% cut in price leads to a 10% increase in sales.
What is the price elasticity of demand?

11 If a good has a price elasticity of −3 it is price inelastic. True or false?

12 If demand is price elastic then a fall in price increases revenue. True or false?

13 If a good is price inelastic then a fall in price increases revenue. True or false?

14 A Rolls Royce car is likely to have a *low/high* price elasticity and a *low/high* income elasticity. Choose the correct options.

15 Milk is likely to have a *low/high* price elasticity and a *low/high* income elasticity. Choose the correct options.

What did you score?

Now check your answers, giving yourself one mark for each one correct.

If you scored:

12–15   **Congratulations! You clearly know these topics well. Now move on to the next section.**

8–11   **This is quite a good score. It shows that you know some sections of these topics. However, there are some areas you need to revise. Why not look over the material again before moving on to the next section?**

Less than 8   **This is less than half marks. You obviously need to revise these topics again.**

Marking exam answers

Question
Discuss the value of the concept of the price elasticity of demand to the marketing department of a major supermarket. **(10 marks)**

Marked answer
The price elasticity of demand measures how sensitive demand is to changes in price. **C** A good may be price elastic (value greater than 1) or price inelastic (value less than 1). **C**

If the marketing manager knows that a good is price elastic she can lower the price and know that sales revenue will increase. Although the price is lower per item, sales will increase so much that the overall revenue rises. The change in sales is greater than the change in price (in percentages). **AN** If demand is price inelastic then a higher price increases revenue. Therefore price elasticity is very important to help decide whether to put the price up or down. **E**

Examiner's comment

A good general answer. It shows a good understanding of the concept of price elasticity and shows how this information may be of use to a marketing manager when setting prices. However there are two areas that could be improved.

1 The answer is not set in the context of a supermarket. It would have been better to have thought about how a supermarket manager in particular would use this information.

2 There is little discussion of the value of the concept. The answer says it is useful (and sets out to prove this) but does not question the value of the concept.

Mark: Content: 2/2 Application: 0/2 Analysis: 3/3 Evaluation: 1/3 Total: 6/10

Your chance to mark

Mark the answer to this question, using the marking scheme on page xvii.

Question

Analyse two factors that might determine the price elasticity of a particular brand of car.

(7 marks)

Student answer

The price elasticity measures changes in demand compared to changes in price. The more sensitive demand is to price, the more price elastic it is.

The price elasticity of demand for a car will depend on how customers perceive it. If they think it is very special (perhaps because of its design or because it has special features such as low fuel consumption) then the price elasticity will be low.

It will also depend on who is paying for the car. Some people have their cars bought for them by their companies and so they do not really care what the price is (although the company might). In this case the car is price inelastic for the individual if it is a brand the company wants to buy.

Mark: Content: _ /2 Application: _ /2 Analysis: _ /3 Total: _ /7

Now look at page 112 to compare your comments and marks with the examiner's.

2.1 Costs, profit and break-even analysis

Content

- **Fixed costs:** costs that *do not* change with output, for example rent.
- **Variable costs:** costs that *do* change with output, for example material costs.
- **Total costs** = Fixed costs + Variable costs
- **Direct costs:** costs that can be directly linked to a product, individual, department or division and that change with output.
- **Indirect costs:** costs that cannot be directly linked with a product, individual, department or division and that do not change with output. Also called **overheads**.
- **Revenue:** the value of sales (equal to Price × Quantity sold). Also called Total Revenue or Sales or Turnover.
- **Profit** = Revenue − Total costs
- **Break-even:** the minimum level of output at which revenue equals total costs.
- **Contribution per unit** = Price per unit − Variable cost per unit
- **Total contribution** = Contribution per unit × Number of units sold

Analysis

- Break-even is the measure of the minimum number of units that need to be sold in order for revenue to cover costs exactly. If more units than this are sold the firm makes a profit; if a firm sells less than break-even it makes a loss.
- Break-even analysis can be used to analyse the effects of changes in price, variable costs, fixed costs or output.
- The contribution per unit contributes towards fixed costs.
- Break-even output can be calculated by:

$$\frac{\text{Fixed costs}}{\text{Contribution per unit}}$$

- Simple break-even analysis depends on some simplifying assumptions, for example that all units can be sold for the same price and that the variable costs per unit stay constant. In reality, these assumptions may not be accurate. For example, the price may have to fall in order to sell more, or the variable costs per unit may fall with larger orders. However, making such assumptions makes it quicker to produce the break-even chart, allowing the firm to make decisions more quickly.
- Break-even analysis can show the level of profits for any level of sales. It can also predict the impact on profits at any level of sales if the price is changed. However, the key question is still "How many units will the firm sell?". Break-even analysis cannot answer this. It can show how many you want to sell to break even or to make a desired profit, but it can't tell the firm whether it will actually sell this number.

Evaluation

- The value of break-even analysis depends on the accuracy of the underlying assumptions. For example, if the firm is estimating the profits at different levels of sales, the value of the results depends on the accuracy of the estimates of variable costs and revenue.

Examiner's advice

When answering exam questions on costs, profit and break-even analysis:

- Make sure you know how to calculate break-even, but also make sure you know why it is an important concept. Why does it matter if the break-even output increases or decreases?

- Remember that break-even is an output. It measures how many units have to be sold for revenue to cover costs.

Break-even maths

There are two key types of break-even questions.

- **Type A questions:** calculate the break-even output or the profit or loss at different levels of output.
  - ☐ To calculate break-even output, use the equation:

    $$\frac{\text{Fixed costs}}{\text{Contribution per unit}}$$

  - ☐ To calculate the profit or loss at different outputs, calculate the total contribution (Contribution per unit × Number of units) and deduct the fixed costs.

Worked example 1

Selling price = £30; variable costs per unit = £20; fixed costs = £50 000

Contribution per unit = Selling price per unit – Variable costs per unit

$$= £30 - £20 = £10$$

Break-even output $= \dfrac{£50\,000}{10} = 5000$ units

Profit/loss at 2000 units:

Total contribution = £10 × 2000 = £20 000

  Profit or loss = £20 000 − £50 000 = –£30 000

Profit/loss at 6000 units:

Total contribution = £10 × 6000 = £60 000

  Profit or loss = £60 000 − £50 000 = +£10 000

- **Type B questions:** plot a break-even chart.
  1 Calculate the break-even output (using the method for **Type A**).
  2 Decide on the maximum output. (You may be given this; if not, for simplicity double the output you calculated for break-even.)
  3 Plot Total revenue. Plot the first point at (0, 0) (when you sell nothing the revenue is £0). Then look at the maximum output and work out the total revenue for this output (using Price × Output). Plot this point on your graph. Join your two points with a straight line.
  4 Plot Total costs. At 0 output the only costs are the Fixed costs, so plot this point. At maximum output the Total costs are Variable costs + Fixed costs. Calculate the variable costs using Variable cost per unit × Output. Then add on Fixed costs to calculate Total costs.
    Plot this point on your graph. Join your two points with a straight line.
  5 Mark Break-even output at the output where Revenue = Total costs.
  6 To show profit and loss for a given output, find the revenue and cost associated with that output and mark on the vertical distance between the two. If costs are higher than revenue, it is a loss. If costs are lower than revenue, it is a profit.

Worked example 2

Selling price = £50; variable costs per unit = £20; fixed costs = £6000

1 Break-even output = $\dfrac{6000}{50 - 20}$ = 200 units

2 Maximum output is 400 units (if you are not given a value for maximum output, double the value you calculated for break-even).

3 Total revenue at 400 units = 400 × £50 = £20 000. Plot the points (0, 0) and (400, £20 000) and join them with a straight line.

4 Fixed costs at 0 output are £6000.
   Total costs = Variable costs + Fixed costs
   At 400 units, Variable costs are £20 × 400 = £8000
   So Total costs = £8000 + £6000 = £14 000
   Plot the points (0, £6000) and (400, £14 000) and join them with a straight line.

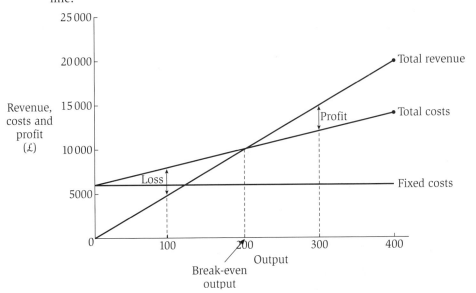

Practice questions

 Maths questions

1 The selling price per unit is £15. The variable cost per unit is £5. Fixed costs are £10 000.

   a What is the contribution per unit?

   b What is the break-even output?

2 Fixed costs are £15 000. The variable cost per unit is £2.
   What are the total costs when output is 2000 units?

3 Fixed costs are £4000. Variable cost per unit is £6. The selling price per unit is £12.
   For an output of 5000 units, find:

   a the revenue

   b the total costs

   c the profit.

4 The selling price is £50 per unit. The variable cost per unit is £20. The fixed costs are £6000.

   a What is the contribution per unit?

   b What is the break-even output?

5 In a restaurant the variable costs per meal are £5 and the selling price is £20. Complete the table below:

Output per week	Fixed costs (£)	Variable costs (£)	Total costs (£)	Total revenue (£)	Profit (£)
0	15 000	0	15 000		
500	15 000	2500		10 000	
1000			20 000		
1500					
2000				40 000	

Diagram questions

1 Label the axes and the lines on this break-even chart.

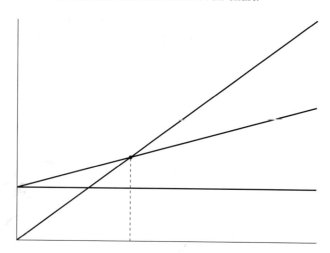

2 a Label the axes and lines on this break-even chart.
b Draw in a line to illustrate the effect of increasing the price.
c Mark on the old and new break-even outputs.

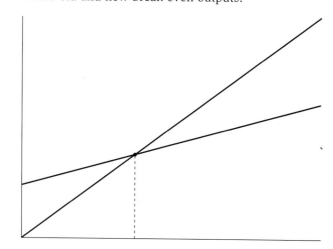

3 Label the axes and lines on this break-even chart.
Draw in a line to illustrate the effect of decreasing the variable cost per unit.
Mark on the old and new break-even outputs.

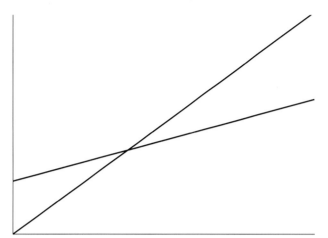

4 On this break-even chart, identify and mark the profit and loss at:
a 100 units   **b** 300 units   **c** 400 units

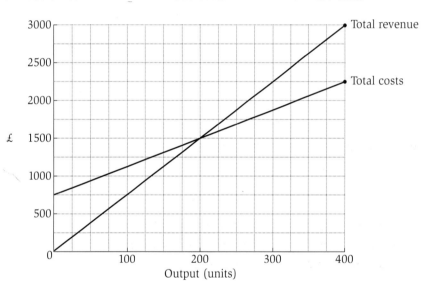

Quick questions

1 Interest repayments on a loan are an example of a fixed cost. True or false?

2 Break-even is the level of output at which the total revenue equals the fixed costs. True or false?

3 Total revenue = Price × ....

4 Total cost = ... costs + ...costs

5 Contribution per unit = Selling price − .... cost per unit

6 Profit = Total .... − Total ....

7 If fixed costs increase, the break-even output will *increase/decrease*.
Choose the correct option.

8 If the variable cost per unit falls, the break-even output will *increase/decrease*.
Choose the correct option.

9 When the output level is zero, no revenue is generated. True or false?

10 Fixed costs must still be paid when output is zero. True or false?

11 An increase in price will shift the total cost line. True or false?

12 If the selling price per unit falls, the break-even output will *increase/decrease*. Choose the correct option.

13 Fixed costs never change. True or false?

14 All indirect costs are fixed. True or false?

15 Indirect costs can also be called o.....................

What did you score?

Now check your answers, giving yourself one mark for each one correct.

If you scored:

12–15 Congratulations! You clearly know these topics well. Now move on to the next section.

8–11 This is quite a good score. It shows that you know some sections of these topics. However, there are some areas you need to revise. Why not look over the material again before moving on to the next section?

Less than 8 This is less than half marks. You obviously need to revise these topics again.

Marking exam answers

Question

Sope Martin is considering setting up as a hairdresser. Discuss the possible value of break-even analysis in helping Sope to make a decision whether or not to set up her business. **(10 marks)**

Marked answer

Sope needs to know whether her idea is feasible or not **C**. This means she needs to know whether the hairdresser's can make a profit or not. Break-even analysis can help here, because she can work out how many customers she will need for her revenue to cover her total costs. **AN** **AP** She can then estimate how many customers she thinks she will get and decide if she will make a profit and how much she will make. From this she can decide whether it is worth it or not. **AN**

However the break-even chart will not actually tell her how many customers she will get; this will be an estimate. If she gets this estimate wrong then she will not estimate her profits or losses correctly. So ultimately the value of the analysis depends on the accuracy of her forecast. **E**

Overall, break-even analysis can help in making decisions – in Sope's case whether or not to open a hairdresser's. However, its value depends on how accurate her estimates are – not only of the number of customers but also of the expected costs. This may depend on how much research she has done in advance, but for a new business the number of customers may be difficult to predict because there is no previous data for this shop. **AP** **E**

Examiner's comment

A well structured answer. It considers the case for, the case against and then produces some form of judgement about the need for accurate data.

A good response, although it could have shown greater analysis of the value of break-even.

Mark: Content: 2/2 Application: 2/2 Analysis: 2/3 Evaluation: 3/3 Total: 9/10

Your chance to mark

Mark the answer to this question, using the marking scheme on page xvii.

Question

Examine two ways in which a football club might reduce its break-even level
of output.

(7 marks)

Student answer

Break-even is the level of output that a firm must sell for its revenue to cover costs.
A firm can reduce the break-even by raising the price or cutting costs. Cutting costs
means reducing fixed or variable costs such as players' wages. If costs are lower you
don't need to sell as much to pay for these, so break-even is lower. On the break-even
chart the cost line will come down.

Mark: Content: _ /2 Application: _ /2 Analysis: _ /3 Total: _ /7

*Now look at page 113 to compare your comments and marks with the
examiner's.*

2.2 Cash flow and finance

Content

C

- **Cash flow:** the difference between cash inflows and cash outflows.
- A **cash-flow forecast** estimates future cash inflows and outflows.
- **Factoring:** a form of cash flow management. A firm that sells items on credit is paid immediately by another organisation called a debt factor. When customers pay for their goods, this money goes to the debt factor rather than the firm that sold the products. The debt factor provides cash for firms and then has to wait to be paid by their customers. The debt factor charges firms for this service. (This service can also be called "invoice discounting".)
- **Sale and leaseback:** when a company sells an asset (for example, a building) and then rents it back.
- **Working capital:** the day-to-day finance in a business.
- **Ordinary share:** represents part ownership of a company. Each share carries one vote; the more shares a shareholder owns, the more votes he or she has.
- **Debenture:** a way of borrowing money. A firm sells a debenture and agrees to pay interest on it. The initial borrowing is repaid on an agreed date.
- **Loan:** when a firm borrows money for a set period of time and meanwhile pays interest. At the end of the time period the loan is repaid. A loan is a form of external finance.
- **Overdraft:** a short-term form of external borrowing. A bank can ask for an overdraft to be repaid at any moment.
- **Venture capital:** money lent to small to medium sized firms in return for interest payments and shares in the business. (Also known as risk capital.)
- **Internal sources of finance:** money raised from within the business. Sources include profit, working capital and the sale of assets.
- **External sources of finance:** money raised from outside the business. Sources include ordinary share capital, loan capital, overdrafts, debentures and venture capital.
- **Revenue:** the value of items sold, regardless of whether the cash has been received for these.
- **Costs:** the value of items used up in producing the goods sold, regardless of whether these have been paid for yet in cash.

Analysis

A

- By constructing a cash-flow forecast, a firm can estimate times when it may need to organise an overdraft, or times when it may have too much cash and could be investing it elsewhere.
- If the cash outflow is greater than cash inflows, the firm may have cash flow problems and need to organise an overdraft.
- Cash and profit are different! For example, if an item is sold on credit it counts as revenue and can therefore generate profit; however the cash inflow has not yet occurred. Therefore sales and revenue can be high even if cash inflows are not.
- A cash-flow forecast estimates the future cash inflows and outflows. (It is forward looking.) The profit and loss statement shows the organisation's income and expenses over the last year, published by the company in its annual report. (It is backward looking.)

- Sale and leaseback helps improve a firm's cash flow in the short term; in the long term the costs of renting are likely to be higher than if you own the item yourself.
- People buy shares to become part owners of a business. They may receive a proportion of the profits via dividends. If the business is successful, the value of their shares may also increase.
- When deciding between internal and external finance, a firm must consider:
  - ☐ what is available (for example, the bank may not be willing to lend to the company)
  - ☐ what it will cost (for example, the rate of interest)
  - ☐ whether it will affect its day-to-day ability to function (for example, if assets are sold).
- When raising finance, a firm should only sell assets it does not need. It is important to remember that once they are sold, assets cannot be used and cannot be sold again.
- Profit measures the excess of revenue over costs. It rewards the owners for their investment and encourages people to invest in the business, for example to build up stocks or capital.
- Improving working capital control may include:
  - ☐ chasing up money owed (debtors)
  - ☐ giving shorter credit terms so that less is owed
  - ☐ delaying paying suppliers
  - ☐ not having as much money tied up in stock.

Evaluation **E**

- The importance of cash compared to profit depends on your perspective. To survive and be able to pay the bills, a firm must have sufficient cash flow. However, for it to be worthwhile being in business you want the revenue to be bigger than the costs; there needs to be a profit for the activities to be worthwhile. On a day-to-day basis cash is essential to survive, but over the long term you need profit to provide rewards for the owners and funds for investments.
- The amount of cash a firm needs to hold depends on its likely outgoings and on how easily it can get cash at short notice.
- The interest a firm pays on a loan depends on the risk involved (if it is very risky the lenders are likely to charge more) and on how long the firm needs to borrow for.
- How long customers are given to pay for a purchase depends on the industry. For example, to join a health club you may pay in advance; in a café you pay when you buy; when you buy a computer you may pay over a few months.

Examiner's advice

When answering exam questions on cash flow:

- Remember that cash and profit are not the same – do not use the words as if they are the same.
- Remember that you may make a profit and yet have cash flow problems (for example, if you have sold items but not yet been paid for them).

Cash flow and finance maths

- **Constructing or completing a cash-flow forecast**
  To do this you will usually need the following information:
  - ☐ Opening balance: the amount of cash the firm starts with at the beginning of the period
  - ☐ Cash inflows: the cash received each period, for example from sales
  - ☐ Cash outflows: the cash leaving the business each period, for example to buy materials
  - ☐ Net cash flow: the difference between cash inflows and cash outflows for this period. For example, if cash inflows are £500 and cash outflows are £200, there is a positive cash flow of £300.
  - ☐ Closing balance: the amount of cash that the firm has at the end of a period. Remember that the closing balance in period 1 is the opening balance in period 2. For example, if you have £50 in your bank at the end of January, then this is the amount you start with at the beginning of February.

  A cash-flow forecast is concerned with the inflow and outflow of cash. For example, if a firm sells an item in January but is paid for it in February, you must enter the cash inflow in February.

Worked example

	June (£000)	July (£000)	August (£000)
A Opening balance	100	110	140
B Cash inflows	30	50	20
C Cash outflows	20	20	30
D Net cash flow (B − C)	10	30	(10)
Closing balance (A + D)	110	140	130

Note: At the end of June the firm has £110 000 so this is the opening balance for July. In August the cash outflows exceed the inflows so the net cash flow is negative (written in brackets).

Practice questions

Maths questions

1 Complete this cash-flow forecast.

	January (£)	February (£)	March (£)	April (£)
Opening balance	200	210		
Cash inflows	50	70		50
Cash outflows	40		60	80
Net cash flow (inflows − outflows)	10	20	(10)	
Closing balance	210			

Diagram questions

Methods of raising finance are listed below.

Write each method under the correct heading in the table.

    a selling shares   **b** loan   **c** profits   **d** sale and leaseback

Internal	External
Profits	loan

Quick questions

1 Purchasers of ordinary shares have one vote, regardless of how many shares they own. True or false?

2 Raising money through selling shares is an example of an internal source of finance. True or false?

3 Debentures are an external source of finance. True or false?

4 A short-term borrowing from a bank, which can be called in at any time, is called an ....

5 To raise money a firm may sell its buildings and then rent them back. This is called .... and ....

6 A holder of a debenture is an owner of a company. True or false?

7 The profits paid out to shareholders are called d......................

8 On which of these forms of finance does a firm pay interest?

    a shares   **b** profits   **c** loans

9 A firm sells an item for £200 on credit. The item costs £150 to produce. These costs are paid in cash. As a result of this transaction:

    a What is the profit?

    b What is the cash flow position?

10 Which one of the following would improve a firm's cash flow position?

    a Suppliers insisting on being paid more quickly.

    b An extension of the credit period given to customers.

    c A decrease in the interest rates on a firm's borrowing.

    d An increase in raw material prices.

11 Raising finance using debtors as collateral is known as f...............

12 The day-to-day finance in the business is called KIOWRGN TAIAPLC Unscramble the letters.

13 To improve cash flow you could chase your debtors to pay more quickly. True or false?

14 Shareholders are paid rewards out of a firm's profits. These are called NVISEDDDI. Unscramble the letters.

15 Which of the following is more of a short term than a long term source of finance?

    a loan   **b** overdraft   **c** share capital   **d** debenture

What did you score?

Now check your answers, giving yourself one mark for each one correct.

If you scored:

12–15   **Congratulations! You clearly know these topics well. Now move on to the next section.**

8–11   **This is quite a good score. It shows that you know some sections of these topics. However, there are some areas you need to revise. Why not look over the material again before moving on to the next section?**

Less than 8 **This is less than half marks. You obviously need to revise these topics again.**

Marking exam answers

Question

Analyse two ways in which a small manufacturing company could raise the finance necessary to purchase new equipment. **(7 marks)**

Marked answer

A firm may raise money by borrowing it from a bank. **C** This could be in the form of a loan. **C** The company would then have to pay interest on the loan. Alternatively a company could sell shares, whereas a sole trader could not. **AP** This does not involve interest payments but the firm may have to pay dividends and reduce future profits. **AN**

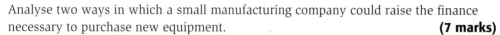

Examiner's comment
A rather brief answer. It identifies two appropriate ways of raising finance but there is only limited analysis and application.

Mark: Content: 2/2 Application: 1/2 Analysis: 1/3 Total: 4/7

Your chance to mark
Mark the answer to this question, using the marking scheme on page xvii.

Question

Fendi Ltd sells photocopiers to small businesses. It is suffering from cash flow problems at the moment. Discuss two ways in which the firm could improve its cash flow. **(10 marks)**

Student answer

To improve its cash flow a firm could delay paying suppliers. This would mean it was holding on to its cash for longer. However, whether this was a good idea or not would depend on the reaction of suppliers. It might be that the suppliers decide not to supply any more under these conditions, in which case Fendi needs to think about how easy it is to get parts from elsewhere. Alternatively Fendi might change the terms for customers, for example insisting on being paid within 4 weeks not 6 weeks. This would bring in the cash more quickly. However, whether or not this was a good idea would depend on whether customers accepted the new conditions or switched to a new photocopier supplier. If they were likely to switch because there were lots of other firms selling photocopiers and offering longer credit terms, then this could be a bad idea.

Overall, the possible reaction of the people you are dealing with must be considered before making any changes, because if you don't things may get worse. There's no point insisting that customers pay quickly if you actually lose all your customers!

Mark: Content: _/2 Application: _/2 Analysis: _/6 Evaluation: _/3 Total: _/10

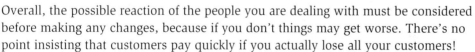

Now look at page 113 to compare your comments and marks with the examiner's.

2.3 Budgeting, cost centres and profit centres

Content

- **Budget:** a quantifiable financial target, set for costs or for revenue.
- **Variance:** a difference between the budgeted figures for costs or revenue and the actual outcomes.
- **Favourable variance:** when actual profits are higher than the budgeted figure; for example, because the actual costs are lower than budgeted costs and/or the actual revenue is higher than budgeted revenue.
- **Adverse variance:** when profits are lower than the budgeted figure; for example, the actual costs are higher than budgeted and/or the actual revenue is lower than the budgeted figure.
- **Zero budgeting:** when the budget is set to zero at the beginning of the budgeting process and managers have to justify every item they want included.
- **Cost centre:** a part of a business where costs can be allocated and measured, for example a product, division, individual or region.
- **Profit centre:** a part of a business where costs *and* revenues (and therefore profits) can be allocated and measured, for example a product, division, individual or region.

Analysis

- A budget may motivate staff by providing them with a target.
- A budget can be part of a review process to see how a manager has performed.
- A budget can help with cash flow planning. By setting targets, managers can help plan expected cash inflows and outflows.
- A budget helps to coordinate managers' activities, since managers must discuss their plans when setting it.
- Setting budgets can cause problems: subordinates may feel that they are being told what to do, or that the targets are too difficult to meet. Superiors may feel that subordinates are trying to set targets that are easy to meet and want the targets to be more demanding.
- Creating cost and profit centres helps managers to become aware of the financial consequences of their actions. It helps to ensure that they focus on costs and revenues.
- Creating cost and profit centres gives managers control over costs and revenues in their area, which may help motivate them.
- The maintenance department creates costs but not revenues. It could be a cost centre but not a profit centre.
- Brand X generates revenue and incurs costs. It could be a profit centre.
- Even if the variances are favourable, a manager will still want to know why the actual outcomes are different from what was expected. Firms need to try to understand what is happening more effectively.

Evaluation

- The value of budgets depends on how they are set (agreed between the superior and subordinate or simply imposed), whether they are achievable and whether or not they are kept to.

■ The value of budgets depends on how they are used. In some organisations managers welcome them as a way of discussing future plans and the resources necessary. Budgets can also be seen as a way of delegating authority to subordinates, who then have to achieve their targets. In other organisations budgets are seen as a control mechanism to limit staff actions, for example to make sure they do not overspend.

Examiner's advice

When answering exam questions on budgeting, cost centres and profit centres:
■ Make sure that you know the limitations and problems as well as the benefits. Although the concept of budgeting may seem appealing, in practice it can be difficult.
■ Remember that budgets can be set for revenue as well as for spending.
■ Make sure you understand the difference between an adverse and a favourable variance. If costs are higher than budgeted this is adverse; if actual revenue is higher than budgeted this is favourable.

Budgeting maths

■ **Variance**

You may be given a firm's budgeted and actual figures and asked to calculate the difference between them and decide whether it is a favourable or adverse variance (see column 4 in the table below).

You may also be asked to suggest why a particular variance might have occurred (see column 5 in the table below).

Alternatively, you might be given the variance and the budgeted figures and be asked to calculate the actual figures from these.

The table below gives some examples of budgeted and actual figures, the calculations of variance and comments on the results.

Item	Budget (£)	Actual (£)	Difference (£)	Comment
Sales revenue	200	220	20 favourable variance (because the actual profits are greater than expected)	This might be because you had more customers than expected.
Labour costs	60	50	10 favourable variance (because the actual profits are greater than budgeted)	This might be because the job took less time than expected.
Material costs	90	105	15 adverse variance (because the actual profits are less than budgeted)	This might be because the materials cost more than expected or because we used more of them than expected.
Profits (Revenue minus Costs)	50	65	15 favourable variance (because the actual profits are higher than expected)	This is because the benefits of higher revenue and lower labour costs than expected exceeded the unexpected increase in material costs.

Practice questions

 Maths questions

1   Complete the budget below. State whether any variance is "favourable" or "adverse".

Item	Budgeted figures (£)	Actual figures (£)	Variance (£)
Sales revenue	20 000	15 000	
Labour costs	5000		2000 favourable
Material costs	1000	2000	1000 adverse
Other costs	2500	2500	
Profit			

2   Complete the table.

Item	Budgeted figures (£)	Actual figures (£)	Variance
Sales revenue	40 000		Actual sales revenue is 10% higher than budgeted
Labour costs	8000		Actual labour costs are 25% higher than budgeted
Material costs	20 000		Favourable variance of £2000
Profit	12 000		

3   Complete the table.

Item	Budgeted figures (£)	Actual figures (£)	Variance
Sales revenue	12 000		Actual sales revenue is £1000 higher than budgeted
Labour costs	4000		Actual labour costs have an adverse variance of 20% higher than budgeted
Material costs	6000		
Profit	2000		Profit has a favourable variance of £1500

Diagram questions

1   Here are six statements about the difference between budgeted and actual costs and revenues. For each statement, decide whether it is an adverse or favourable variance and write it in the correct section of the table.

   a   Higher labour costs than budgeted

   b   Lower rent than budgeted

   c   Lower sales revenue than budgeted

   d   Higher tax bill than budgeted

   e   Lower marketing spending than budgeted

   f   Lower material costs than budgeted

Adverse variance	Favourable variance

2   Tick the correct circle.

	True	False
This year's budget must always be bigger than last year's.	○	○
A profit centre involves measuring revenues as well as costs for a part of the business.	○	○
A budget involves setting a non financial, qualitative target.	○	○
A budget involves setting a financial, qualitative target.	○	○

Quick questions

1   A .... is a quantifiable financial target.

2   A budget is always backward looking. True or false?

3   A firm forecasts that its sales revenue will be £10 000. In fact it is £8000. Is this a favourable or adverse variance?

4   A budget is a financial statement produced to show the government. True or false?

5   A firm estimates that its labour costs will be £4000. In fact they turn out to be £3000. Is this a favourable or adverse variance?

6   Zero budgeting means that managers are not allowed to spend any money. True or false?

7   Managers never spend more than their budgets. True or false?

8   If we set targets for the revenue and the costs for a particular department this is known as a .... centre.

9   Budgeted labour costs are £20 000. Actual labour costs are £30 000. Is this a favourable or adverse variance?

10   Budgeted sales revenue is £50 000. Actual revenue is £66 000. Is this a favourable or adverse variance?

11   All firms have budgets. True or false?

12   An unexpected increase in sales is likely to lead to a favourable variance. True or false?

13   Budgets can be set for revenues as well as costs. True or false?

14   An unexpected increase in staff overtime work because of new orders is likely to lead to a favourable variance in labour costs. True or false?

15   The cleaning department of an organisation is likely to be a *cost/profit* centre. Choose the correct option.

What did you score?

Now check your answers, giving yourself one mark for each one correct.

If you scored:

12–15   **Congratulations! You clearly know these topics well. Now move on to the next section.**

8–11   **This is quite a good score. It shows that you know some sections of these topics. However, there are some areas you need to revise. Why not look over the material again before moving on to the next section?**

Less than 8 **This is less than half marks. You obviously need to revise these topics again.**

Marking exam answers

 Question

Discuss two reasons why the actual costs may be higher than the budgeted costs for a manufacturer of shoes. **(10 marks)**

 Marked answer

This could be because the supplier of leather has increased its prices and so materials (such as the leather) cost more than anticipated. **C AP** Or it might be because the employees who make the shoes demand more pay and so labour costs are higher than budgeted. **C AP AN** Or it could be because rent has gone up in the factory where the shoes are made. **C AP** Or it could be because other things like electricity are more expensive than expected, perhaps because the firm used more than it thought it would. **C** So overall there are many things that could have caused the costs to be more than the firm thought they would be, because life in business is unpredictable. **E**

> ### Examiner's comment
> This answer identifies many different types of costs such as rent and labour. It also tries to relate them to the type of business (for example, referring to leather). However it does not develop the points very successfully or very fully. As a result analysis is limited.
>
> The candidate gives more than **two** reasons. There is no extra credit for this and the candidate penalises him/herself by using up valuable time. In this situation it is usually better to select your best two points, rather than write about all three.
>
> **Mark: Content: 2/2 Application: 2/2 Analysis: 1/3 Evaluation: 1/3 Total: 6/10**

Your chance to mark

Mark the answer to this question, using the marking scheme on page xvii.

 Question

Discuss the possible value of introducing budgets into a fast growing organisation.

(10 marks)

 Student answer

Budgets stop people spending so much and so this is good because they won't overspend. This means the firm does not waste profit, although if it is growing fast the firm may not care as much because it may be making lots of profit already. Budgets make people think about money and how it is spent. This is useful because otherwise people just spend and don't care. Much better to constrain people so they are controlling what they do.

Mark: Content: _ /2 Application: _ /2 Analysis: _ /3 Evaluation: _ /3 Total: _ /10

Now look at page 114 to compare your comments and marks with the examiner's.

2.4 Investment appraisal, balance sheets and profit and loss statements

Content

- **Investment appraisal:** the assessment of possible investment projects to decide which one(s) should go ahead. Techniques include payback and Accounting (or Average) Rate of Return.
- **Payback:** measures the time it takes for an investment to recover its initial costs.
- **Accounting Rate of Return (ARR):** measures the average profit per year as a percentage of the initial investment. Also called Average Rate of Return.

$$\text{ARR} = \frac{\text{Average annual profit}}{\text{Initial investment}} \times 100 = \%$$

- **Balance sheet:** shows the value of a firm's assets at a particular moment in time. It also shows how the finance has been raised to acquire the assets.
- **Net assets:** = Total assets − Current liabilities
  = Fixed assets + Current assets − Current liabilities
  Also called **assets employed**. The assets employed will always equal the capital employed.
- **Return on Capital Employed:** a profitability ratio.

$$\text{Return on capital employed} = \frac{\text{Net profit}}{\text{Capital employed}} \times 100 = \%$$

- **Gearing ratio:** shows what proportion of long-term funds are borrowed.

$$\text{Gearing ratio} = \frac{\text{Long-term liabilities}}{\text{Capital employed}} \times 100 = \%$$

- **Current ratio:** a liquidity ratio

$$\text{Current ratio} = \frac{\text{Current assets}}{\text{Current liabilities}}$$

Typically the value of this ratio is around 2.

- **Acid test ratio:** $= \dfrac{\text{Current assets} - \text{Stock}}{\text{Current liabilities}}$

A liquidity ratio; the typical value is around 0.8.
- **Profit and loss statement:** shows the revenue, costs and profits of a business over a given period (usually one year).
- **Assets:** anything that provides a benefit to an organisation.
- **Fixed assets:** items with a value (in money terms) that are owned by a firm and are expected to provide a benefit for more than one year.
- **Current assets:** items with a value (in money terms) that are owned by a firm and are expected to provide a benefit for less than one year.
- **Working capital** (also called net current assets): the day-to-day finance in the business.
  Working capital = Current assets − Current liabilities
- **Liabilities:** debts an organisation owes.
- **Current liabilities:** debts that have to be repaid within 12 months, for example an overdraft.
- **Long-term liabilities:** debts that do not have to be repaid within 12 months, for example a long-term loan.

- **Capital employed:** measures the long-term sources of finance within the business, for example long-term liabilities, retained profits and issued share capital.
- **Window dressing:** legitimate accounting techniques used to make the accounts look flattering.
- **Revenue:** the value of goods sold.
- **Costs:** the value of items used up in the process of producing and selling the goods sold.
- **Profit:** Revenue − Costs

Analysis

- If a firm is concerned about its cash flow position, it will want a project with a quick payback.
- If a firm is assessing a project on purely financial grounds, the higher the accounting (average) rate of return the better.
- Investment appraisals are based on expectations of future costs and revenues. Therefore there are risks associated with the results, which are based on forecasts and assumptions.
- Financial statements and forecasts such as balance sheets and investment projections only show financial costs and benefits. When making a decision, a manager may also take into account non-financial factors, such as employee morale, the environmental impact or ethical concerns.
- When deciding which project to choose, a manager may consider the initial investment (it may not be possible to raise the necessary finance) and how reliable the estimates are for each project.
- A firm interested in profits will want to have as high a return on capital employed as possible.
- A high gearing ratio may involve high interest payments. This may cause problems if income falls, as the firm may find it difficult to meet the interest payments. However, if a firm does not borrow it may miss business opportunities.
- Typically the current ratio is around 2. This means that the current assets are twice as big as the current liabilities. If the current ratio is too low, the firm may be illiquid.
- Typically the acid test ratio is around 0.8. This means that the current assets, less stocks, cover about 80% of the current liabilities.
- A firm's profit may be paid out to the owners (for example, as dividends to shareholders) or retained for investment.

Evaluation

- The value of published accounts depends on how recently they were produced and what window dressing techniques have been used.
- Published balance sheets and profit and loss statements are backward looking. Managers also need to consider what might happen in the future before making a decision.
- The value of investment appraisal techniques depends on the quality of the underlying data. This depends on how the numbers were estimated, who estimated them and how far into the future they are trying to predict.

- Ratios such as return on capital employed, gearing, current ratio and the acid test ratio, can be used to analyse accounts. However, they have limitations. For example:
  - ☐ Balance sheets reflect a firm's position at a specific moment in time – not necessarily on a typical day.
  - ☐ Investors will be interested in the future, but published accounts reflect the past position of a firm.
  - ☐ Non-financial factors, such as employee morale, may be important but do not show in the financial accounts.

Examiner's advice

When answering exam questions on investment appraisal, balance sheets and profit and loss statements:

- Remember to look at the date of any financial information you are given. It may be very out of date and therefore of limited value for forecasting the future.
- Remember the figures used in investment appraisal are mainly estimates. You need to know how they have been calculated.

Investment appraisal maths

The table shows the projected net cash inflows for two projects over four years.

Year	Projected net cash inflows (£m)	
	Project A	Project B
0	(10)	(8)
1	4	3
2	6	3
3	6	4
4	4	4

- **Calculating payback**

  Payback is the time it takes to recover the initial investment.

  For project A:
  Initial investment is £10m.
  Inflows = 4 (year 1) + 6 (year 2).
  Payback is 2 years.

  For project B:
  Initial investment is £8m.
  After 2 years inflow is £6m, so we still need £2m more.
  £4m is expected in year 3, so £2m is expected in the first half of year 3.
  So payback = $2\frac{1}{2}$ years or 2 years 6 months.

- **Calculating Accounting Rate of Return (ARR)**

  1. Calculate the Net profit (= Total expected inflows − Initial investment).

  2. Calculate the average annual profit $\left(= \dfrac{\text{Net profit}}{\text{Number of years}}\right)$.

  3. The ARR is given by $\dfrac{\text{Average annual profit}}{\text{Initial investment}} \times 100$

Worked example

For the table above:

		Project A	Project B
1	Net profit (£m)	$4 + 6 + 6 + 4 - 10 = 10$	$3 + 3 + 4 + 4 - 8 = 6$
2	Average annual profit (£m)	$\dfrac{10}{4} = 2.5$	$\dfrac{6}{4} = 1.5$
3	Accounting Rate of Return	$\dfrac{2.5}{10} \times 100 = 25\%$	$\dfrac{1.5}{8} \times 100 = 18.75\%$

On this basis the firm would choose project A, because it has a quicker payback and a higher rate of return.

■ Calculating working capital

Working capital = Current assets − Current liabilities

Current assets = Stocks + Debtors + Cash

Examples of current liabilities are: an overdraft, creditors, tax due, dividends due.

Worked example

You are given the following data on a company's finance.
Calculate the working capital.

Stock	£500
Cash	£200
Debtors	£300
Overdraft	£400
Creditors	£100
Dividends due	£ 50
Tax due	£100

Working capital = $(500 + 300 + 200) - (400 + 100 + 50 + 100)$
$= 1000 - 650$
$= £350$

Practice questions

Maths questions

1 The table shows the projected net inflows for two projects over three years.

Year	Projected net cash inflows (£m)	
	Project A	**Project B**
0	(20)	(50)
1	10	40
2	15	40
3	13	12

a Calculate the payback period and Accounting (Average) Rate of Return for both projects.

b On the basis of your results in **a** which project would you choose? Explain your answer.

2 The initial investment in a project is £50m. The expected Accounting Rate of Return is 20%.
What is the expected average annual profit?

3 The current assets of a business are £100m.
Its long-term liabilities are £200m.
Its current liabilities are £40m.
Its fixed assets are £600m.
What is the firm's working capital?

Diagram questions

1 These items may appear on a balance sheet.
   Write them in the correct circles.

   a Cash

   b Overdraft

   c Long-term loan

   d Factory

   e Buildings

   f Tax due to be paid

   g Machinery

   h Debtors (money owed by customers)

   i Creditors (money owed to suppliers)

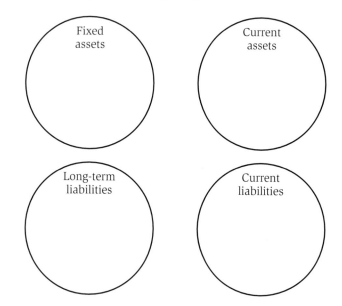

2 Complete this balance sheet.

   Balance sheet as at 1 June 200X

	£m
Fixed assets	42
Current assets	20
Current liabilities	
Net assets	*50*
Long-term liabilities	12
Issued share capital	
Reserves	20
(e.g. retained profit)	
Capital employed	

3 Complete this profit and loss statement

	£m
Revenue	
Cost of sales	5
Gross profit	4
Overheads	3
Operating profit	

Quick questions

1 The process of assessing an investment project is known as Investment ASARPAPLI. Unscramble the letters.

2 The time it takes for a project to recover its initial investment is called the .... period.

3 Which of these is a fixed asset?
  a cash
  b overdraft
  c loan
  d factory

4 Which of these is a current asset?
  a money owed by customers (debtors)
  b money owed to suppliers (creditors)
  c debenture
  d a factory

5 Working capital is the same as:
  a Capital employed
  b Current assets + Current liabilities
  c Current assets − Current liabilities
  d Fixed assets

6 Which of these is a current liability?
  a issued shares
  b overdraft
  c debtors
  d cash

7 If a firm were choosing an investment project on financial grounds alone, it would prefer the payback to be *short/long* and the Accounting (average) Rate of Return to be *high/low*. Choose the correct options.

8 To calculate profit we can use the equation R............... − C..........

9 Some profit is paid out to the owners (for example, as dividends); some is kept by the business. The profit kept by the business is known as "R............ profit".

10 A 5-year loan is a form of:
  a current asset
  b fixed asset
  c long-term liability
  d current liability

11 Which one of the following is a fixed asset?
  a machinery
  b creditor
  c debtors
  d loan

12 Which of the following statements is true?
  a A balance sheet shows a firm's financial position over one year.
  b A balance sheet shows a firm's financial position at a given moment in time.
  c A balance sheet shows a firm's revenues and costs.
  d A balance sheet shows a firm's cash inflows and outflows.

13 The value of a company's shares is always the same as the value of the company on the balance sheet. True or false?

14 Revenue measures:
   a The value of a firm's assets.
   b The value of a firm's cash inflow.
   c The value of a firm's sales.
   d The value of a firm's costs.

15 Stocks held by a firm are an example of:
   a fixed assets
   b current assets
   c costs
   d current liabilities

What did you score?

Now check your answers, giving yourself one mark for each one correct.

If you scored:

12–15 **Congratulations! You clearly know these topics well. Now move on to the next section.**

8–11 **This is quite a good score. It shows that you know some sections of these topics. However, there are some areas you need to revise. Why not look over the material again before moving on to the next section?**

Less than 8 **This is less than half marks. You obviously need to revise these topics again.**

Marking exam answers

Question

Discuss the factors a manager of a carpet business might consider before investing in a new factory.

(10 marks)

Marked answer

An investment can be risky and so a manager will want to try and reduce this risk by doing some research first. **C** The sorts of things the manager may want to know include the expected Accounting Rate of Return (ARR). This measures the annual profits of the firm in relation to initial investment. Before borrowing money or using funds which could be used elsewhere, the manager will want to make sure the ARR is high enough to be worth bothering with. **AN** If the ARR is low a firm may not think the investment is worthwhile because the money could be better used elsewhere. **AN** However, the numbers must be treated with caution because they are based on expectations of what might happen, so there is a risk that they may be wrong. **E** The firm might also consider the payback period, that is how long it will take to recover the initial investment. **C** A project with a quick payback and a high Average Rate of Return is likely to be financially attractive to a firm. **AN** But non-financial factors should not be forgotten because these might affect the decision (for example, if the factory would damage the local environment or wildlife, the project may not go ahead). Sometimes these non-financial factors can play an important role in the decision. **E**

Examiner's comment

Generally a good answer that shows a good grasp of the subject matter. The candidate clearly understands the concept and techniques of investment appraisal. The candidate also highlights the limitations of payback and Average Rate of Return, such as the need to consider non-financial factors as well.

The main weakness in the answer is the fact that the candidate does not relate the answer to the context of a carpet business and the purchase of a new factory.

Mark: Content: 2/2 Application: 0/2 Analysis: 3/3 Evaluation: 2/3 Total: 7/10

Your chance to mark

Mark the answer to this question, using the marking scheme on page xvii.

Question

To what extent are the published accounts of a firm useful to a potential investor?

(10 marks)

Student answer

The published accounts include the balance sheet, which shows assets. Assets are important because you own them and if you don't have them you don't own things. The better the business is doing, the more it can afford and the more assets it has. If the assets of a firm are shrinking this is not so good so you wouldn't want to invest. You want to invest in a firm with big assets.

Also from the accounts you can see the firm's profits. If its profits are falling then you don't want to be part of that business and you would not invest. On the other hand if its profits are rising you want to be part of it, so you get big dividends.

So looking at the accounts can tell you whether or not you will make any money.

Mark: Content: _/2 Application: _/2 Analysis: _/3 Evaluation: _/3 Total: _/10

Now look at page 115 to compare your comments and marks with the examiner's.

3.1 Management structure and organisation

Content

- **Organisational structure:** the way in which jobs are organised within a firm, for example who reports to whom.
- **Functional organisational structure:** when jobs are grouped by the nature of the work. For example, there may be a Marketing department, a Finance department, a Human Resource Management department and an Operations department.
- **Matrix structure:** when work is organised so that individuals have two or more bosses. Individuals work on a project and report to their functional boss (for example, the marketing manager) and also the project leader.
- **Corporate culture:** the values, attitudes and beliefs of employees within an organisation; "the way we do things around here".
- An individual with **authority** has the legitimate power to complete a task.
- **Accountability:** when an individual is answerable for the successful completion of a task.
- **Mission:** sets out the overall goals of the organisation, its values and where it wants to compete. If the mission is written down it is known as a "mission statement".
- **Objectives:** quantifiable targets, that is clear measurable targets with an agreed timescale. For example "to increase profits by 20% over two years".
- **Responsibility:** the obligation to complete a task.
- **Centralisation:** the extent to which authority is held at higher levels in an organisation.
- **Decentralisation:** the extent to which authority is passed down the organisation.
- **Span of control:** the number of subordinates *directly* responsible to a superior.
- **Levels of hierarchy:** the number of layers of authority in an organisation.
- **Delayering:** removing levels of hierarchy in an organisation.
- **Delegation:** when a manager entrusts a subordinate with a task.
- **Consultation:** when a manager who is making a decision asks employees for their views and suggestions.
- **Leadership:** the ability to influence others to pursue a desired good voluntarily.
- **Leadership style:** the way in which people are managed. For example, are employees simply told what to do or are they asked for their opinions?
- **Quality circles:** voluntary groups at work that meet to discuss how to improve quality in their work area (for example, ways of reducing the number of defective products).
- **Kaizen groups:** teams that work to find ways of continually improving the way things are done.
- **Management by objectives:** an approach that attempts to coordinate activities by ensuring each employee is set a target. Objectives are cascaded down the organisation from the senior staff to the junior employees.

Analysis

- Better organisational design leads to quicker, cheaper decision making.
- Management by objectives can help to coordinate activities. Objectives also motivate staff.
- Delegation may motivate employees. It also frees up management time to focus on more strategic issues.
- A narrow span of control is likely to give greater control over subordinates. This reduces the risk of errors but may demotivate staff due to excessive interference.
- Many levels of hierarchy may create opportunities for promotion and enable a firm to have smaller spans of control. However, it also increases costs and may mean that communication is distorted, as messages have to pass through many levels of the organisation.
- Centralisation enables senior managers to keep control. These people may have more experience and make better decisions, taking into account the needs of the organisation as a whole. However, centralisation may mean that the organisation does not respond well to local market conditions and that local managers feel demotivated because they do not make decisions.
- Delayering can cut costs by removing a layer of managers, but it can increase stress in the managers who are left, because they have additional duties and wider spans of control.
- A functional organisational structure brings together all the specialists in one particular area (such as marketing), so they share ideas, experiences and resources. However, it may not encourage much cooperation and communication between functions (for example, between marketing and production).
- Matrix management helps coordination within the firm by cutting across functional boundaries. However, it may lead to confusion where staff have two bosses.
- Consultation may make employees feel more involved in the organisation. It may lead to better decisions, because more ideas are generated. However, the process may be slower than decision making without consultation.

Evaluation

- There is no "correct" structure. The best organisational structure for a firm will depend on, for example, the challenges facing the firm, the environment, the task and the employees.
- The effectiveness of delegation depends on the ability of the subordinates and whether the subordinates have the resources they need to carry out the task.
- Corporate culture is not easy to change. It may take time to change it and staff are likely to resist changes to the way they do things at the moment.
- The value of management by objectives depends on whether employees are simply told what to do or whether they are involved in setting their own objectives. It also depends on whether the objectives are realistic and whether the firm provides sufficient resources for objectives to be achieved.
- The value of consultation depends on employees' attitude to it and whether they have the necessary knowledge and skills to contribute effectively.

3.1 Management structure and organisation

Practice questions

Diagram questions

1 What is the span of control of the Managing Director in this organisational chart?

2 The diagram below is an example of a .... organisational structure.

3 The diagram below is an example of a .... organisational structure.

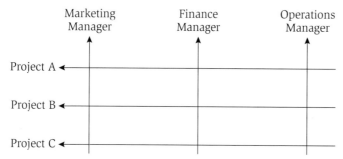

4 How many levels of hierarchy are there in this organisational chart?

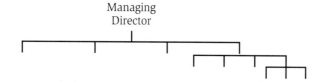

Quick questions

1 If most decisions in the organisation are made at a senior level, the organisation is *centralised/decentralised*. Choose the correct option.

2 Asking employees for their opinion is known as *consultation/delegation/kaizen*. Choose the correct option.

3 If the number of levels of hierarchy in an organisation is reduced, this is likely to *increase/decrease* the span of control. Choose the correct option.

4 Reducing the number of levels of hierarchy in an organisation is called d...................

5 From an organisational chart it is *not* possible to identify:
  a A manager's span of control
  b The levels of hierarchy
  c The amount of authority a manager has
  d Reporting relationships.

6 An objective is:
  a A long-term plan
  b The values, attitudes and beliefs of employees
  c A quantifiable target
  d A short-term plan.

7 Consultation involves:
  a Telling employees what to do
  b Letting employees decide what they want to do for themselves
  c Asking employees for their opinions
  d A wide span of control.

8 An approach that continually tries to find better ways of doing things is called ZAKEIN. Unscramble the letters.

9 MBO is a system of coordinating employees' actions within a firm. These letters stand for M..................... B... O...................

10 A narrow span of control means:
  a A superior has relatively few people reporting to him or her directly.
  b A superior has a lot of people reporting to him or her directly.
  c The organisation must be very small.
  d The organisation must be very big.

11 An organisational structure in which individuals have two or more bosses is known as a TAXIMR structure. Unscramble the letters.

12 The overall goals of an organisation are usually stated in its NSMSIOI statement. Unscramble the letters.

13 Entrusting a subordinate with a task is known as d................

14 Which of the following is the best example of an effective objective?
  a To increase sales by 20% over 3 years.
  b To enter a market by selling low price goods.
  c To increase profits a lot.
  d To become the most respected producer of ice cream in the UK.

15 Which statement best describes a centralised organisation?
  a All decisions are made by junior managers.
  b Relatively little authority is dispersed throughout the organisation.
  c All decisions are taken in one place.
  d Subordinates are not allowed to decide anything.

What did you score?

Now check your answers, giving yourself one mark for each one correct.

If you scored:

12–15 **Congratulations! You clearly know these topics well. Now move on to the next section.**

8–11 **This is quite a good score. It shows that you know some sections of these topics. However, there are some areas you need to revise. Why not look over the material again before moving on to the next section?**

Less than 8 **This is less than half marks. You obviously need to revise these topics again.**

Marking exam answers

Question

Discuss the possible consequences of increasing the span of control of managers in a company with declining profits. **(10 marks)**

Marked answer

The span of control measures the number of subordinates directly responsible to a superior. **C**

The span of control may depend on:

- The skills of the subordinates
- The nature of the task
- How good the communication system is.

If the span of control is large this may mean:

- The superior is overworked
- The subordinates do not receive enough direction
- There is not effective control. **C**

Examiner's comment

This answer begins with a definition of span of control, which is a good way to start. However, after this the candidate wastes time by explaining what the span of control may depend on. This is not asked for and the candidate is penalising him or herself by failing to address the question properly.

In the last section the candidate identifies some points that may be relevant, but uses bullet points, so the points are not really developed.

Also, the question asked about "increasing" the span rather than "a large span", which may be different. Lastly there is no attempt to evaluate.

Mark: Content: 2/2 Application: 0/2 Analysis: 0/3 Evaluation: 0/3 Total: 2/10

Your chance to mark

Mark the answer to this question, using the marking scheme on page xvii.

Question

Ransom Ltd is a glass manufacturer. The company has been doing badly and many managers are leaving the business. Discuss the possible benefits of introducing a management by objectives approach at Ransom Ltd. **(10 marks)**

Student answer

The management by objectives system can motivate and provide direction. It can also coordinate and help control. It depends on the objectives themselves. If they are unrealistic they will not motivate because no one will bother to try and achieve them. Also it depends whether people are involved in setting the targets. If you are just told what to do you will probably not do it. If you are asked what you should do you may be more interested.

In this case a management by objectives system may help managers to focus on key targets (agreed with superiors). This could help improve their performance and that of the firm as whole. Also, with clear targets managers may be more willing to stay and this could save on recruitment and training costs and improve motivation.

Mark: Content: _/2 Application: _/2 Analysis: _/3 Evaluation: _/3 Total: _/10

Now look at page 115 to compare your comments and marks with the examiner's.

3.2 Motivation

Content

- **Motivation:** an individual's desire to act in a certain way. For example, employees may be motivated to improve product quality.
- **F.W. Taylor:** associated with Scientific Management. Taylor believed that there was "one best way" of doing something. His technique involved observing the way a job was done, developing a better way, introducing it and monitoring the results. He believed managers should manage and subordinates should implement. By following the "one best way", employees could produce more and be rewarded financially for the higher output. This would motivate them, because according to Taylor, people are motivated by money.
- **Elton Mayo:** associated with the Hawthorne Effect. The Hawthorne Works study highlighted the importance of meeting employees' social needs at work. Employees were motivated by the fact that managers were listening to them. Mayo also highlighted the importance of groups and informal leaders at work.
- **Abraham Maslow:** developed Maslow's Hierarchy of Needs: physiological, safety/security, social, esteem (ego), self-actualisation. To motivate, managers have to offer appropriate rewards to match an employee's needs. For example, they could offer money for physiological needs, a long-term contract for security needs, teamwork for social needs, a new job title for esteem needs and greater authority for self-actualisation needs.
- **Frederick Herzberg:** identified "hygiene" and "motivator" factors at work. **Hygiene factors** prevent dissatisfaction. They are factors extrinsic to the job (outside of the job), for example the basic pay, colleagues and the company rules. **Motivator factors** are intrinsic to the job (related to the job), for example, the degree of authority in the job, the variety in the task and the opportunities for more challenge at work.
- **Herzberg** also distinguished between "motivation" and "movement". **Movement** is when individuals do something because they have to (for example, to keep their jobs). **Motivation** means that individuals do something because they want to.
- **Job enrichment:** when jobs are made more satisfying by giving employees greater challenge and authority in their work.
- **Job enlargement:** when more tasks of a similar level of responsibility are added on to a job.
- **Job rotation:** individuals move from one job to another, which provides variety at work.
- **Empowerment:** when employees are given greater control over their working lives – they have more control over what they do and when they do it.
- **Authoritarian leadership:** when a manager tells employees what to do. Communication is one way.
- **Democratic leadership:** when a manager listens to employees and involves them in the decision-making process. Communication is two way.
- **Paternalistic leadership:** when a manager acts like a "father" to employees; the manager makes decisions acting in what he or she believes is the best interests of employees.
- **Laissez faire leadership:** when managers let employees get on with the work and make decisions for themselves.
- **McGregor's Theory X:** describes managers who believe that employees dislike work and need to be controlled and coerced.
- **McGregor's Theory Y:** describes managers who believe that employees want to work and can be creative if managed and rewarded properly.

- **Piecework:** a payment system where employees are paid according to the amount they produce, for example a set amount per unit.
- **Performance related pay:** a payment system where employees are set targets (usually on a number of criteria) and the rewards they receive relate to how far these targets are achieved.
- **Profit share:** employees receive a proportion of the firm's profits.
- **Employee share ownership:** individuals working within the organisation have part-ownership of the business.
- **Fringe benefits:** rewards employees receive in addition to their usual salary or wage, for example company car, pension and health insurance.
- **Salary:** employees receive a fixed amount of money per month.
- **Team-based management:** employees work in groups and the team makes decisions, rather than one individual.
- **Single status:** when all employees in the organisation have the same employment conditions and reward schemes. For example, all employees are paid salaries and they all use the same canteen.

Analysis **AN**

- Motivation can lead to greater productivity (greater output per worker), which can reduce the cost per unit and therefore increase the profit per unit. Motivation can also improve the quality of the work done.
- A manager's leadership style can influence employees' motivation and thus the performance of the business.
- To be effective, financial incentives should be cost-effective, motivate employees towards employers' goals, and be easy to administer and understand.
- To motivate, the rewards a firm offers must match the differing needs of employees.
- Some rewards may simply prevent dissatisfaction. To motivate staff you may need different types of rewards. "Hygiene" and "motivator" factors are not the same.
- The fact that individuals do something does not mean that they are motivated. They may be doing it only because they have to, in which case they will lack commitment. "Movement" and "motivation" are not the same thing.
- The theorists highlighted that there are different factors that may motivate people at work.
- Remember that a firm may not be able to offer some rewards (for example, it may not be able to afford higher pay).
- Pay may be most successful as a motivator in terms of meeting lower level needs. Higher level needs depend more on the job itself.

Evaluation **E**

- Motivation does not in itself guarantee a better performance. You also need to consider factors such as the technology available, the training, the machinery and the individuals' abilities.
- Motivation does not guarantee an increase in productivity. For example, shop assistants cannot easily influence the number of customers they serve – this depends on how many people come in to the shop in the first place.

- The "right" leadership style depends on many factors, for example how long you have to complete the task, the attitude of employees (both individually and when they work in a group) and the risk involved.
- Motivating people is not always easy. It is not always obvious what people want and sometimes the firm cannot offer it (for example, the firm cannot afford it, or there are no promotion opportunities).
- The power of money to motivate may depend on:
  - ☐ how much money an employee has already
  - ☐ how much you are offering them
  - ☐ what everyone else around them is earning
  - ☐ what employees have to do to earn it.
- Whether employees welcome empowerment depends on how they perceive it. Some may see it as exploitation – a way of getting them to work harder.
- Different pay schemes have different uses. Piecework may be a good way of getting employees to produce more, but it may not encourage them to focus on quality or develop new skills for the future.
- It is not a question of whether one motivational theorist is right and the others are wrong. All the motivational theorists bring their own insight into motivation. Some of these may be more or less appropriate for different people at different times.

Examiner's advice

When answering exam questions on motivation:

- Don't always wait to be asked directly about the theorists – refer to them whenever you are writing about motivation. If you are looking at the impact of change on employees' motivation, try to relate it to a theorist.
- Many students write about Theory X type and Theory Y type *employees*; in fact McGregor was writing about the *managers'* attitude to employees. McGregor *did not* say some employees were lazy; he said that some managers act as if they think that some employees are lazy. This is an important difference.
- Be careful how you use the word "motivation". When people are motivated they choose to behave in a certain way because they want to. If people do things because they are forced to, because they are scared they will lose their pay if they don't, or because they think they will lose their job if they don't, this is not motivation.

Practice questions

Diagram questions

1   The diagram shows Maslow's Hierarchy of Needs.
     Label the different levels of need.

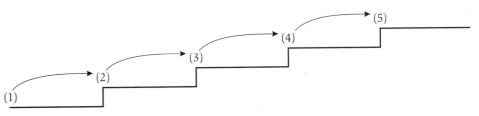

2 Think of six factors at work that Herzberg would label *either* "Hygiene" factors *or* "Motivators". Write each factor in the correct circle.

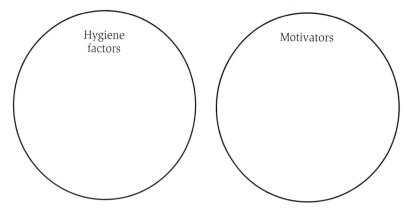

3 Listed below are various assumptions managers can make about employees. For each statement, decide whether it illustrates the Theory X or Theory Y approach, and write it under the correct heading.
  a Workers need to be controlled and forced to work.
  b Workers are motivated by money.
  c If trusted, workers will behave responsibly.
  d Employees have a desire to contribute.
  e Workers have no desire to contribute to decisions.
  f Employees want job satisfaction, just like managers.

Theory X	Theory Y

4 a Which type of payment system does this diagram illustrate?

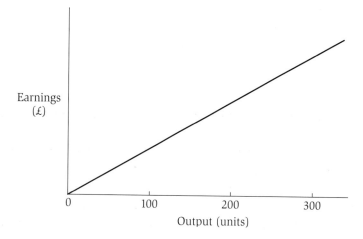

  b The firm offers a higher, bonus pay rate once a target of 200 units is achieved. Draw a line on the diagram to show this.

Quick questions

1 Taylor believed that people came to work to fulfil their social needs. True or false?

2 Under a salary scheme, individuals are paid *by the hour/per unit produced/a fixed amount per year/an amount linked to profits.* Choose the correct option.

3 A manager who simply tells employees what to do can be described as *authoritarian/democratic/paternalistic.* Choose the correct option.

4 Herzberg distinguished between "Hygiene" factors and "............" factors.

5 If managers assume that employees want to contribute to the organisation and are capable of using their initiative, this is typical of McGregor's *Theory X/Theory Y.* Choose the correct option.

6 If managers invite employees to contribute to the decision-making process this is an *authoritarian/democratic/paternalistic* management style. Choose the correct option.

7 *Maslow/Mayo/Taylor/Herzberg* undertook the Hawthorne Works study, which highlighted the fact that employees often react favourably if management listen to them. Choose the correct option.

8 According to Herzberg, "hygiene" factors can prevent employee dissatisfaction but do not motivate. True or false?

9 When an employee is paid a set amount for every unit produced, this is called ....

10 Which of the following is *not* one of Herzberg's "motivators"?
  a Basic pay
  b Increased authority
  c Greater variety in the task
  d The opportunity for career development

11 F. W. Taylor is associated with TSCCIFIIEN management. Unscramble the letters.

12 Changing a job to make it more motivating, by providing the job-holder with greater authority, is called job e.....................

13 Telling employees what to do is an example of *authoritarian/democratic* management. Choose the correct option.

14 If employees are concerned about dangerous working conditions, what need does this relate to in Maslow's Hierarchy of Needs?

15 If people respond to having a new, more important sounding job title, what need is being fulfilled in Maslow's Hierarchy of Needs?

What did you score?
Now check your answers, giving yourself one mark for each one correct.
If you scored:

12–15   **Congratulations! You clearly know these topics well. Now move on to the next section.**

8–11   **This is quite a good score. It shows that you know some sections of these topics. However, there are clearly some areas you need to revise. Why not look over the material again before moving on to the next section?**

Less than 8   **This is less than half marks. You obviously need to revise these topics again.**

Marking exam answers

Question

The managers of TrendZ, a clothes shop, are worried about the morale of their staff. Discuss the ways in which they might try to motivate their staff. **(10 marks)**

Marked answer

Many staff in clothes shops are part-timers. **C** **AP** They are often students or people who need extra money. The name TrendZ makes it sound as if it is a shop aimed at younger people, so this may be somewhere students will want to work. **AN** **AP** Students are often working to earn some money to pay for holidays, music, or going out. Perhaps the managers should look at the pay rates compared to other shops in the area, because this might be important. **AN** **AP** The staff may be dissatisfied because they are earning less than their friends elsewhere. **C** The managers might also want to think about what has changed over time – why are the staff dissatisfied now? **C** However, the best thing might be to ask the shop assistants what they want. **E** It is not always easy to motivate people because you need to know what they want. **E** Maslow's Hierarchy of Needs shows that different people want different things and that managers have to offer different rewards. For example, for security needs staff may need to know they have a long-term job (not likely to be so important if people are just working for some extra money part time); **AN** for self-actualisation needs people may want the chance to take control of something (again not necessarily very important for part-timers). Motivation is not simple. **E**

Examiner's comment

The answer starts well by thinking clearly about this type of business and who might be working here (part-timers). The answer is quite thoughtful: "The name TrendZ makes it sound as if it is a shop aimed at younger people". It makes a good comment about the need to look around and see what others are doing and think about what has changed over time. This is quite reflective. It is also important to find out what staff want. The answer refers quite well to a theorist (Maslow), recognising that different people will be motivated by different rewards, which is judgemental.

Mark: Content: 2/2 Application: 2/2 Analysis: 3/3 Evaluation: 3/3 Total: 10/10

Your chance to mark

Mark the answer to this question, using the marking scheme on page xvii.

Question

Hugo Carboni has just taken over as boss of the Melton Design company. Discuss the factors that might influence Hugo's management style. **(10 marks)**

Student answer

How you manage depends on the culture of the firm. The culture will affect the way you are expected to behave and often the way you are rewarded. Start behaving in an "odd" way and your boss or colleagues may not be happy. So if the general style is to be democratic, you obviously will feel pressurised to do the same. Although you may be strong enough to resist this, many of us "go with flow" because it makes life easier. So the management style is often the same in a business – you do what others do.

Mark: Content: _/2 Application: _/2 Analysis: _/3 Evaluation: _/3 Total: _/10

Now look at page 116 to compare your comments and marks with the examiner's.

3.3 Human resource management

Content

- **Workforce planning:** a process of estimating a firm's human resource requirements by considering the future demand for and supply of labour.
- **Recruitment and selection:** the process of identifying the need for a job, defining the requirements of the position and the job holder, advertising the position to attract applicants and choosing the most appropriate person for the job.
- **Internal recruitment:** an organisation searches within the firm for someone to fill a vacancy.
- **External recruitment:** an organisation searches for someone from outside the firm to fill a vacancy.
- **On the job training:** when employees learn how to do a job by actually doing it; they are trained as they undertake the task.
- **Off the job training:** when employees undertake training away from the exact place that they work. For example, attending a training course at a local college, or attending a lecture or workshop within the firm but away from where they work each day.
- **Induction training:** training for employees when they first join an organisation or start a new job. This training introduces them to the job and the organisation, for example who does what, what resources are available, company policy.
- **Selection:** the way that a firm chooses between applicants, for example by interview or testing.
- **Market failure:** in this context, this means when firms are unwilling to train staff because employees may leave, wasting the firm's investment.
- **Poaching:** when one firm attracts employees away from another firm.
- **Labour targets:** specific human resources objectives for an organisation, for example to recruit a certain number of people for a certain outlet by a certain time.
- **Redundancy:** when the job no longer exists (for example, when a business or parts of a business have closed down).
- **Dismissal:** when an employee's employment is terminated because he or she cannot do the job properly (for example, because they are incapable of doing the task to a satisfactory standard).
- **Labour turnover:** a measure of the number of staff who have left over a given period compared to the average number employed during the same period, calculated as a percentage.

$$\text{Labour turnover} = \frac{\text{Number of people leaving over a given period}}{\text{Average number employed during the period}} \times 100$$

- **Retirement:** when employees leave an organisation because they have finished their working career.

Analysis

- Human Resource Management (HRM) recognises that employees are a resource of the organisation; as such they have to be carefully selected, managed and maintained, just like any other resource.
- A firm's human resource requirements depend on:
  - ☐ The firm's overall strategy. (Is it expanding or shrinking? Is it opening new shops in the South or in the North?)
  - ☐ The labour market. (Are there enough workers ready to work in the area?)
  - ☐ Changes to the existing workforce. (How many will leave due to ill health or retirement?)

- Workforce planning leads to action plans, such as recruiting staff, training them, or transferring them to other parts of the organisation.
- Effective workforce planning ensures that a firm has the right number of employees with the right skills and attitudes at any moment in time.
- To encourage staff to stay after they have been trained, some organisations have a pay scheme in which the rewards grow considerably once employees have been with the firm for several years.
- Training can improve employees' skills, make employees aware of new approaches and can be motivating.
- High labour turnover can be expensive due to recruitment and training costs.
- High labour turnover may be due to poor pay, poor management, poor conditions or better opportunities elsewhere.

Evaluation

- Workforce planning can help ensure a firm has the right staff at the right time with the right skills and attitudes. However, its effectiveness depends on the quality of the forecasts and the ability to attract the staff required. Sudden changes in the working environment, or labour shortages, may make planning difficult.
- The value of training depends on the cost, the perceived benefits and the impact on skills, motivation and attitude. It also depends on whether the employee stays with the firm.
- The aim of human resource management is *not* to "make people happy". The aim is to maximise individuals' contribution to the organisational objectives. People may be very happy but they may not actually be helping the firm to achieve its goals.
- The importance of HRM is increasing as people are recognised as a key resource. The skills, knowledge and experience of employees are a vital asset and a source of competitive advantage for a firm; they have to be carefully managed.
- The extent to which high labour turnover is a problem depends on how easy (and how expensive) it is to recruit new staff.

Examiner's advice

When answering exam questions on human resource management, remember:

- Training is not always desirable – it depends on whether employees need to learn about new skills or new ideas and how they react to the training programme. In some cases training can be ineffective and therefore a waste of money.
- People need to be developed as a resource – they are an investment and need to be managed effectively. This is not always easy, because employees' interests and objectives may be different from the organisation's.
- It can be difficult to recruit staff and this can act as a constraint on the firm's activities.
- Firms differ – some will want to invest in long-term training; others will accept a high labour turnover if they feel they can recruit staff easily.

Human resource management maths

Labour turnover = $\dfrac{\text{Number of people leaving over a given period}}{\text{Average number employed during the period}} \times 100$

Worked example

20 people left McCallum's Ltd last year. On average the size of the workforce was 200 people.

What was the labour turnover? $\dfrac{20}{200} \times 100 = 10\%$

Practice questions

Maths questions

1   Five members of staff left Hooter's Nightclub last year. The club employs an average of 80 people.

    What was the firm's labour turnover last year?

2   The labour turnover at Fox's Fast Food is 25% p.a.. On average it employs 400 people. The cost of training new staff is approximately £2000 each.

    a   How many people leave per year on average?

    b   What are the annual training costs for new recruits?

Diagram questions

1   Listed below are various factors in recruitment. For each statement, decide whether it is more likely to refer to "internal" or "external" recruitment and write it under the correct heading.

    a   You know the employee already.

    b   Likely to be more expensive.

    c   Wider choice.

    d   The applicant will already know the firm's culture.

    e   It may motivate staff who see promotional opportunities.

    f   May bring in more experience from outside.

Internal recruitment	External recruitment

2   The recruitment and selection process often include the stages listed below. Put these stages in the correct order in the diagram.

    a   Interview

    b   Advertise the position

    c   Offer employment

    d   Select

    e   Define requirements of job holder

    f   Analyse applications

    g   Identify requirements of the job

Quick questions

1 The initials HRM stand for: H............... R................. M...............

2 When a firm hires people from within the business this is known as i................. recruitment

3 When employees first join an organisation, they may receive i............. training.

4 When employees are trained whilst doing their work, this is called .... training.

5 Fendo Ltd employs 50 staff. On average 20% leave each year. To maintain its workforce, how many staff must be recruited each year?

6 When people leave the business because they have come to the end of their working life, this is called ....

7 When an employee's employment is terminated because he or she cannot do the job properly, this is known as d.............

8 Poaching is when:

   a an employee asks for more money

   b a firm recruits internally

   c a firm uses a salary scheme

   d a firm recruits employees from other firms.

9 Some driving schools now start learner drivers on a simulator. This type of training is known as .... training.

10 When recruiting new staff, an interview is part of the s.................... process.

11 If staff have to leave a firm because there is no longer a job for them, this is called a r.....................

12 Estimating future demand and supply for labour is known as w................. p....................

13 Off the job training means employees are always trained away from the company's premises. True or false?

14 Which one of the following is a legal reason for the "fair dismissal" of employees?

   a They are incapable of doing their job.

   b They are a member of a trade union.

   c They are pregnant.

   d They lied about their qualifications.

15 Compared to internal recruitment, external recruitment is likely to be *quicker/cheaper/offer more choice*. Choose the correct option.

What did you score?

Now check your answers, giving yourself one mark for each one correct.

If you scored:

12–15   **Congratulations! You clearly know these topics well. Now move on to the next section.**

8–11   **This is quite a good score. It shows that you know some sections of these topics. However, there are some areas you need to revise. Why not look over the material again before moving on to the next section?**

Less than 8   **This is less than half marks. You obviously need to revise these topics again.**

Marking exam answers

Question

John O'Connor, the Human Resource Manager at Seafarer Ferry Company, has suggested that the firm should invest more heavily in induction training for staff. Discuss the possible benefits of more induction training for staff working on the ferries.   **(10 marks)**

Marked answer

Induction training is the initial training staff receive when they join an organisation. **C**. This may introduce them to the job and the company, for example its rules, regulations, methods. **C** It may also let you know who is charge of what, what belongs where, how you get things done and so on. All in all it lets you start your job knowing the key things you need to know to do it properly. **C** Without this you waste time finding out things that you could have been told at the start. **AN**

Passengers' lives can be at risk if ferry staff are not trained properly and do not know how to react in various situations. **AP** So better training at the beginning, for example about what to do if there is a problem with the boat, could save lives. **AN** **AP**

Better induction training may also mean better service for passengers. **C** **AP** When customers ask a member of staff where something is they will know, so customers will be more willing to use this company in the future. This can lead to customer satisfaction and more loyalty. You may even be able to charge premium prices and earn higher profit margins. **AP** **AN**

> ### Examiner's comment
>
> A good answer in that the candidate clearly shows a knowledge of induction training. He or she also relates this knowledge very well to the context of ferries. The understanding of the topic is well applied to the context. However, the response lacks evaluation. What do the benefits depend on? Is induction training more important to this industry than to others? The idea that lives could be saved is an important one. This could be compared to other industries where the benefits of induction training may not be so great.
>
> **Mark: Content: 2/2 Application: 2/2 Analysis: 3/3 Evaluation: 0/3 Total: 7/10**

Your chance to mark

Mark the answer to this question, using the marking scheme on page xvii.

Question

Discuss the ways in which effective human resource management might improve the performance of a hotel business.   **(10 marks)**

Student answer

People lie at the heart of any business. If they are managed properly the business will be a success. If people are motivated they work better and make fewer mistakes. They are more productive and this increases the profits of the business. Motivated staff also produce better quality products and this means that there are fewer defects and fewer items have to be re-worked.

Motivated staff turn up to work on time and try much harder, which makes the performance of a firm a lot better than if people are not motivated. In a hotel there are lots of jobs, for example reception staff and cleaners. If these staff are not motivated, things will go badly wrong and then the business is bound to fail. Without motivated staff nothing will work and everything will be bad and go wrong.

Mark: Content: _ /2 Application: _ /2 Analysis: _ /3 Evaluation: _ /3 Total: _ /10

Now look at page 116 to compare your comments and marks with the examiner's.

4 Operations management

4.1 Efficient production

Content

- **Unit costs:** the average cost of making an item.

$$\text{Unit cost} = \frac{\text{Total cost}}{\text{Output}}$$

- **Economies of scale:** when unit costs fall as a firm increases the scale of its operations.
- **Diseconomies of scale:** when unit costs increase as a firm increases the scale of its operations.
- **Capacity:** the maximum output a firm can produce with its existing resources.
- **Capacity utilisation:** the amount a firm is producing at present as a percentage of its maximum capacity.

$$\text{Capacity utilisation} = \frac{\text{Current output}}{\text{Maximum output}} \times 100$$

- **Capacity under-utilisation:** when a firm is producing below full capacity.
- **Rationalisation:** when a firm tries to reduce its costs; often associated with redundancies.
- **Subcontracting:** when a firm uses its facilities to produce on behalf of someone else. For example a cereal company might produce cereal for another firm.
- **Capital intensive:** when the proportion of machines used in the production process is high relative to the proportion of labour, for example in car production.
- **Labour intensive:** when the proportion of labour used in the production process is high relative to the proportion of machines, for example teaching.
- **Productivity:** measures the output produced in relation to the input used. For example, output per hour, output per machine, output per day. The most common measure of productivity is output per worker, known as labour productivity.

$$\text{Labour productivity} = \frac{\text{Output}}{\text{Number of employees}}$$

Measures the output per employee.

- **Job production:** one-off production that produces unique items, for example an architect's design or a painting. Job production provides tailor-made items for customers but is likely to be expensive. The production process is flexible and can be altered to meet customer needs.
- **Batch production:** when groups of items move together in batches from one stage of the process to the next, for example baking bread. The firm can produce a range of different items. However, the process is not as flexible as job production.
- **Flow production:** when items move individually from one stage of the process to the next in a continuous process, for example chemical production. Flow production produces high volumes at a low unit cost but is relatively inflexible.

Analysis **AN**

- Economies of scale may be:
  - ☐ Technical (for example, adopting a production line approach).
  - ☐ Specialisation (for example, specialist managers can be employed to focus on specific areas such as marketing, which can lead to better decision making).
  - ☐ Purchasing (for example, the firm may get discounts for large-scale purchases).
- Diseconomies of scale often occur due to problems with:
  - ☐ Coordination (because there are more departments or people to coordinate).
  - ☐ Communication (because there are more layers of hierarchy or parts of the business are based in different places).
  - ☐ Motivation (employees feel they are less significant within a large organisation and may feel demotivated).
- The capacity of a firm depends on:
  - ☐ the numbers and skills of employees
  - ☐ the state of technology
  - ☐ the level of investment
  - ☐ the production process.
- Capacity utilisation depends on the level of demand. Low levels of demand are likely to lead to low capacity utilisation.
- Productivity depends on:
  - ☐ the training of employees
  - ☐ employees' attitudes and motivation
  - ☐ the machinery and technology used
  - ☐ the quality of management.
- Higher labour productivity means more output per worker. This should reduce the labour cost per unit.
- Flow production is only approprite if there are high levels of demand. It is suited to mass marketing.

Evaluation **E**

- The right scale of production for a firm may depend on the extent to which the firm can benefit from economies and diseconomies of scale.
- The right type of production (job, batch or flow) depends on:
  - ☐ the marketing strategy
  - ☐ the need for flexibility
  - ☐ the resources available
  - ☐ the nature and level of demand (for example, if demand is high for standardised products, flow production may be the most appropriate).
- The right level of capacity depends on the expected level of demand.
- The cost per unit may depend on:
  - ☐ capacity utilisation
  - ☐ productivity
  - ☐ economies of scale
  - ☐ input prices.

Examiner's advice

When answering exam questions about efficient production:

- Remember that operations management can improve the quality of the product, the unit costs and the range and volume of production. However, business success also requires effective marketing, HRM and financial control. For example, you need motivated staff to implement the operations policies effectively, and effective marketing to develop the right products and distribute them.

- Remember to mention all the different forms of economies of scale. Most candidates remember purchasing (or bulk buying) but far fewer remember the other types.

- Define your terms precisely. Economies of scale occur when *unit costs* fall with a larger scale of production, not when *costs* fall.

Efficient production maths

- **Calculating unit costs**

$$\text{Unit costs} = \frac{\text{Total cost}}{\text{Output}}$$

If total costs are £200 and output is 50 units,

$$\text{Unit costs} = \frac{£200}{50} = £4 \text{ per unit}$$

- **Calculating capacity utilisation**

$$\text{Capacity utilisation} = \frac{\text{Current output}}{\text{Capacity}} \times 100$$

If a firm is currently producing 200 units, but its capacity is 400 units,

$$\text{Capacity utilisation} = \frac{200}{400} \times 100 = 50\%$$

- **Calculating labour productivity**

$$\text{Labour productivity} = \frac{\text{Output}}{\text{Number of employees}}$$

If 40 staff make 1000 products per day,

$$\text{Labour productivity} = \frac{1000}{40} = 25 \text{ products per person per day}$$

Practice questions

Maths questions

1 a 20 staff process 100 insurance claims every day. What is their productivity in terms of claims processed per person per day?

   b Each member of staff is paid £400 a day. What is the labour cost to process each claim?

   c New working methods enable staff to boost productivity by 20%. How many claims are now processed each day? What is the cost per claim now?

   d What do your findings suggest about the link between productivity and the labour costs per unit?

2 The capacity of a restaurant is 200 customers per day. The average number of customers per day is 120.
   What is the capacity utilisation of the restaurant?

3 The capacity utilisation of a factory is 80%.
Currently it produces 400 units per day.
What is its total capacity per day?

4 **a** The total costs of production are £4000. Output is 500 units.
What is the cost per unit?

  b Output increases by 20% and costs increase by 10%.
What is the new unit cost?

5 The figures below are for a firm with maximum output 500 000 units per week.

Output	Total costs (£)	Unit costs (£)	Capacity utilisation(%)
100 000	200 000	2	20%
200 000	300 000		
300 000		1.2	
400 000	400 000		
500 000		0.96	100%

  a What is the formula for unit costs?

  b What is the formula for capacity utilisation?

  c Complete the table above.

  d What does the table tell you about the relationship between unit costs and capacity utilisation?

6

Output (units)	Number of employees	Productivity (= output per employee) (units)	Total wage costs (£) (based on employee wage of £300 per week)	Labour cost per unit (£) $\left(= \dfrac{\text{Total wages}}{\text{Output}}\right)$
100	10		3000	
300	15		4500	
500		25		
900			9000	
1000		20		

  a Complete the table.

  b What does the table suggest about the relationship between productivity and the labour costs per unit?

7 Complete the table:

Capacity (units)	Output (units)	Capacity utilisation (%)	Fixed costs (£)	Fixed costs per unit (£) $\left(\dfrac{\text{Fixed costs}}{\text{Output}}\right)$
200	50	25	1000	
200	100		1000	
200	150		1000	
200	200			5

4.1 Efficient production

Diagram questions

1 A firm experienced economies of scale and then diseconomies of scale. On the diagram, draw a line to represent the firm's unit costs.

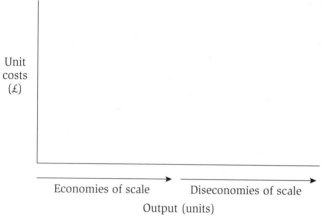

Unit costs (£)

Economies of scale   Diseconomies of scale

Output (units)

2 Listed below are features of different types of production. Write each feature in the correct circle.

  a Can produce tailor-made items

  b Produces high volumes

  c Relatively low unit cost

  d Produces a relatively standardised product

  e Very flexible to customer needs

  f Appropriate for a niche marketing strategy

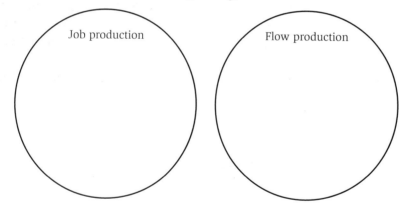

Job production   Flow production

Quick questions

1 Productivity measures:

  a The total output of a business

  b The output of a firm in relation to the inputs used up

  c The total costs of producing

  d The revenue of a firm.

2 If productivity increases, output must increase. True or false?

3 Economies of scale occur when total costs fall as the scale of production increases. True or false?

4 Attempting to reduce costs is called TALRISONIONAATI. Unscramble the letters.

5 One-off production that is flexible enough to meet each individual customer's needs is known as *batch/flow/job* production. Choose the correct option.

6 Under-utilisation of capacity means that the firm is producing less output than it could, given its existing resources. True or false?

7 When a production process is heavily automated, this is a labour intensive process. True or false?

8 The maximum a firm can produce is known as its c...................

9 A production process in which individual items move continuously from one stage to the next is called .... production.

10 Under-utilisation of capacity occurs when:

    a A firm is producing at full capacity.

    b A firm is producing more than 100% of its capacity.

    c A firm is producing less than its maximum output.

    d A firm is producing goods rather than services.

11 When a production process uses a large amount of machinery, this is known as a c................. i.............. process.

12 Flow production produces relatively standardised products. True or false?

13 A firm that produces 10 items, but could be producing 80 items, has a *high/low* capacity utilisation. Choose the correct option.

14 Higher output inevitably means higher sales. True or false?

15 The amount a firm is producing at the moment, compared to the maximum output it can produce given its resources, is called its TCIYACAP TIOULISNATI. Unscramble the letters.

What did you score?

Now check your answers, giving yourself one mark for each one correct.

If you scored:

12–15   **Congratulations! You clearly know these topics well. Now move on to the next section.**

8–11   **This is quite a good score. It shows that you know some sections of these topics. However, there are some areas you need to revise. Why not look over the material again before moving on to the next section?**

Less than 8 **This is less than half marks. You obviously need to revise these topics again.**

Marking exam answers

Question

Charlie Sawyer is a tailor who uses job production, making suits to fit individual customers. Discuss the possible advantages and disadvantages for Charlie of using job production. **(10 marks)**

Marked answer

Job production means one-off or unique production. **C**. Each suit will fit the customer very well and this will lead to greater customer satisfaction. This could mean that Charlie can charge more for his suits, because they fit better than the competition and so give greater customer satisfaction. **AN AP** This allows Charlie to make more profits per item and therefore earn better returns. **AN**

Every customer is a different shape, so if you simply made all suits exactly the same it may be easier and cheaper but the result is that people will have to buy clothes that do not really fit them. **AP AN** It takes more effort to take the time to design each piece of clothing (for example, you have to meet the customer before making the suit, rather than making a load the same and sending them out to other stores to sell). **AN**

However, customers can dictate the things they like and be much more individual. This can be very attractive, provided Charlie can make enough suits in the time available to make enough profit to survive. **E**

Also, producing the suits may need special skills. This could make it difficult to expand the business, because Charlie may not be able to recruit other people with good enough skills to help him. Also it depends on whether customers have the money to pay for such skills and individual items. Some customers may be willing to wear standard suits if they are a lot cheaper (like Marks and Spencer's) and so for them the mass market may be a better option. **E**

Examiner's comment

This is an excellent answer in many ways. The arguments are not always expressed very effectively, but nevertheless the answer is relevant and evaluative. The candidate keeps the answer in the context of suits and discusses both advantages and disadvantages. The answer manages to relate operational issues such as the method of production to human resource issues (recruitment), marketing issues (pricing) and finance (overall profits).

Mark: Content: 2/2 Application: 2/2 Analysis: 3/3 Evaluation: 3/3 Total: 10/10

Your chance to mark

Mark the answer to this question, using the marking scheme on page xvii.

Question

Analyse the economies of scale a restaurant might experience if it increases its scale of operations.

(7 marks)

Student answer

Economies of scale mean it is cheaper to produce.

By getting bigger, a firm might experience several economies of scale such as:

- Technical – larger production is cheaper.
- Financial – it is cheaper to borrow money.

So a restaurant will find it costs less to produce things.

Mark: Content: _ /2 Application: _ /2 Analysis: _ /3 Total: _ /7

Now look at page 117 to compare your comments and marks with the examiner's.

4.2 Controlling operations

Content

- **Stock:** components, raw materials, works in progress or finished goods held by a firm. Stocks may be needed to maintain production or sales.
- **Buffer stock:** the minimum level of stock a firm wants to hold at any time. The buffer stock is kept just in case there are problems with supplies (for example, if a supplier fails to deliver).
- **Opportunity cost:** the benefit the firm foregoes by putting resources into one activity rather than another. For example, money tied up in stocks is not earning interest; if it were in a bank instead it would earn interest.
- **Self-checking:** when employees check their own work, rather than relying on quality control occurring at the end of the process.
- **Benchmarking:** when a firm compares its performance with the standards achieved by other organisations that are performing at a higher level. Ideally firms compare themselves with the best in the world. The aim is to learn from other organisations how to improve performance in specific activities.
- **ISO 9000:** a European quality assurance standard awarded to firms that have a process of quality (previously called BS 5750 in the UK).
- **Stock rotation:** when stocks are moved around to ensure that older stock is used up first (for example, old stock is moved to the front of the shelves).
- **Stock wastage:** when stocks are thrown away, for example because they are out of date.
- **Re-order level:** the level of stock at which a firm orders a new delivery.
- **Lead time:** the time taken from when an order for stock is placed to when the goods actually arrive.
- **The maximum stock level:** the highest level of stock a firm wants to hold.
- **Stockholding costs:** expenses incurred in keeping stocks, for example warehousing costs, security costs, opportunity cost and depreciation.
- **Total Quality Management:** an approach where a firm attempts to build a culture of quality and zero defects throughout the organisation.
- **A process of quality:** quality targets are set, actual performance is measured and when the targets are not achieved appropriate action is taken.
- **Quality control:** a check on quality, based on inspection. It seeks to identify defects once they have occurred.
- **Quality assurance:** set of activities whose purpose is to ensure an organisation is meeting its quality targets. This can help ensure customer satisfaction.

Analysis

- The re-order level for supplies depends on the usage rate and the expected lead time. For example, if the usage rate is high a firm will have a relatively high re-order level.
- The lead time may depend on how long it takes to produce an item and how long to transport it.
- The maximum stock level depends on the opportunity cost and the firm's storage facilities.
- Total Quality Management seeks to reduce costs by reducing the defects in goods produced.
- Self-checking provides employees with more control over their work and may be motivating.

- Improving quality can save costs by reducing the re-working of defective items and avoiding refunds on items that are later returned.
- Improving quality can increase revenue by increasing customer satisfaction.
- By reducing stocks a firm reduces:
  - ☐ opportunity costs
  - ☐ warehousing costs
  - ☐ security costs
  - ☐ depreciation
  - ☐ the danger of goods being damaged or stolen while in storage.
- If a firm runs out of stocks it may not be able to produce and/or it may not have enough items to meet customer demand.
- Benchmarking allows a firm to learn from the best in the world to improve quality and reduce costs.
- A firm with an ISO 9000 award can use this fact in its marketing activities and this may help the firm win contracts. However, it may cost money to develop the systems and keep the records of actual performance and relevant actions taken necessary to win the award.
- Quality control is traditionally associated with inspection at the end of a production line, but a more modern approach involves self-checking by employees at each stage of the process.
- Quality assurance involves a range of activities, including selecting the right supplies and materials, training staff and gaining their commitment, and quality control. If a firm can demonstrate its quality assurance system this may reassure customers.
- Staff may resist the idea of self checking because it involves additional responsibilities and training.
- Staff may resist Total Quality Management because they do not see this as their responsibility.
- The stock usage rate depends on the rate of demand – the higher the level of demand, the more stocks will be used up. A sudden increase in demand will lead to much faster usage. If this is faster than expected it may lead to stocks running out.
- Stocks may be wasted because the firm has over-ordered and the stocks have gone out of fashion or have depreciated (for example foodstuffs are beyond the use-by date).

Evaluation **E**

- The amount of stock a firm holds depends on:
  - ☐ the costs of ordering
  - ☐ the delivery costs
  - ☐ the discounts available for bulk buying
  - ☐ the type of product.
- The value of reducing stocks depends on the opportunity costs and the size of the stockholding costs (for example, security and depreciation).
- Employees may be motivated by self-checking and total quality management. Their motivation may depend on the rewards they are offered and how the new system is introduced.
- The success of Total Quality Management depends on whether employees have the right skills and attitudes.

- Some employees may resist Total Quality Management on the basis that it simply gives them more to do, which they may see as exploitation.
- The value of benchmarking depends on:
  - [ ] who you are benchmarking against
  - [ ] what you are benchmarking
  - [ ] the extent to which other firms are willing to share their methods
  - [ ] the extent to which you can adopt other firms' methods.
- Improving quality has become more important because of increasing levels of competition, greater demands from customers and better technology.
- Total Quality Management is more likely to be successful if the reasons for quality improvement are explained and if the reward systems are linked to better quality.
- A firm is more likely to hold buffer stocks if it expects a sudden increase in demand, if stockholding costs are high or if it expects suppliers' prices to rise.

Examiner's advice

When answering exam questions on controlling operations:

- Remember that the general trend in recent years has been to reduce stock levels. Retailers such as supermarkets now have far more frequent deliveries and manufacturers hold fewer components. However, not all firms have managed to cut down on stocks and there may be reasons why some firms want to hold high levels (for example, if they cannot rely on suppliers to deliver regularly, or want to benefit from bulk-buying discounts). Don't assume that lower stocks are always desirable – if you went shopping and nothing that you wanted was in stock at a particular shop, you might start shopping elsewhere.
- Remember that the importance of stock control will differ from business to business. In manufacturing stocks often represent a major investment, but in services they may be less significant.
- Try to link stock control to issues such as unit costs, competitiveness and the ability to meet customer requirements.

Practice questions

Diagram questions

1 Answer these questions about the stock control chart shown below:
   a What is the re-order level of stocks?
   b What is the buffer stock?
   c What is the lead time?
   d What is the maximum stock level?
   e How much stock is re-ordered each time?
   f How much stock is used up each week?

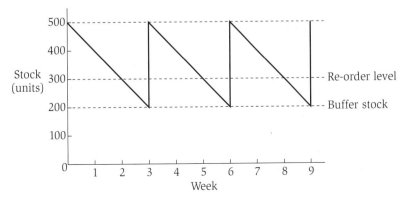

2

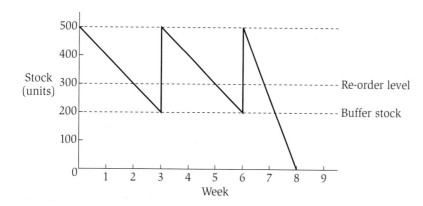

In week 8 the firm has no stocks. Why might this be?

3

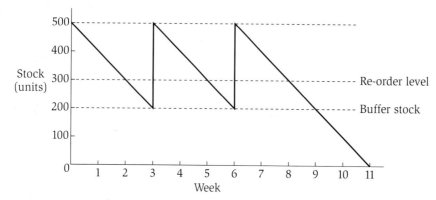

In week 10 the firm has no stocks. Why might this be?

Quick questions

1 Comparing your performance in specific areas with the best in the world is called CHMGENBAKRNI. Unscramble the letters.

2 A quality system that relies on inspection is called "quality ...."

3 The UK award for firms that have a process of quality used to be called BS 5750. The equivalent European award is called ....

4 The minimum stock a firm wants to hold is called the .... stock.

5 The length of time it takes from ordering an item to the item arriving is known as the ....

6 Building a culture of quality is known as TQM. This stands for T.......... Q........... M.....................

7 Which of the following is *not* an example of stocks:
a components
b raw materials
c works in progress
d cash

8 TQM involves employees in decision making. According to Herzberg, involving employees in this way is an example of a m.................... factor.

9 The money tied up in stocks is not earning interest. This represents an o............ c........

10 If stocks depreciate rapidly, firms are likely to want to hold a *higher/lower* stock level. Choose the correct option.

11 When items of stock have to be thrown away because they are out of date, this is known as stock w...................

12 When stock is moved around a store so that the oldest stock gets sold first, this is known as stock r....................

13 Ordering stock in smaller quantities but more frequently may:
  a Decrease administration costs
  b Lead to bulk discounts
  c Increase administration costs.
14 If a firm has an ISO 9000 award, this means that its products are of the highest quality. True or false?
15 If interest rates increase, the opportunity cost of holding stocks *increases/decreases*. Choose the correct option.

What did you score?
Now check your answers, giving yourself one mark for each one correct.
If you scored:

12–15   **Congratulations! You clearly know these topics well. Now move on to the next section.**

8–11   **This is quite a good score. It shows that you know some sections of these topics. However, there are some areas you need to revise. Why not look over the material again before moving on to the next section?**

Less than 8 **This is less than half marks. You obviously need to revise these topics again.**

Marking exam answers

 Question
Analyse the possible benefits of stock control for a company that produces furniture.

(7 marks)

 Marked answer
There are several types of stock. Stocks may be raw materials or works in progress or finished goods. **C** For this firm this may be wood in the factory or finished furniture. **AP A** Holding stocks involves an opportunity cost. **C** Money invested in stocks is not being used elsewhere. By improving the stock control a firm may "free up" more cash, which may be better for the firm's liquidity and it may be able to earn interest on the cash if it puts it in the bank. **AN**

Stock can also be stolen **C**. If you leave lots of items sitting around a factory people may be more tempted to steal them. They may be able to use the wood at home for example or sell it to others. **AP** Better stock control should allow you to keep a better track of the wood and so less may go missing. This means you don't have to replace it by buying more, which saves money. **AN**

> ### Examiner's comment
> This is quite a short but effective answer. It is in context and it shows possible benefits, such as freeing up money and saving on theft.
>
> **Mark: Content: 2/2   Application: 2/3   Analysis: 3/3   Total: 7/7**

Your chance to mark
Mark the answer to this question, using the marking scheme on page xvii.

 Question
Discuss the factors that may determine how much stock a shop holds.   **(10 marks)**

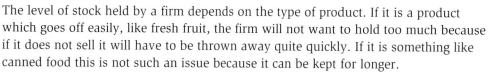

Student answer

The level of stock held by a firm depends on the type of product. If it is a product which goes off easily, like fresh fruit, the firm will not want to hold too much because if it does not sell it will have to be thrown away quite quickly. If it is something like canned food this is not such an issue because it can be kept for longer.

It may also depend on the firm's view of the future – if you think the price of a good is going to increase in the future you may stockpile now. You buy now whilst it is cheaper before it becomes more expensive.

The stock level held will also depend on what you think demand will do. If you think sales are going to increase (e.g. at Christmas) you may stock up now so you can meet customers' orders and avoid customer dissatisfaction.

So there are many factors influencing stock levels, some of which may conflict with each other. Also, conditions change, so a firm should continually review its desired stock levels and may change its policies at different times of the year or in different years depending on conditions such as demand and input prices.

Mark: Content: _ /2 Application: _ /2 Analysis: _ /3 Evaluation: _ /3 Total: _ /10

Now look at pages 117–118 to compare your comments and marks with the examiner's.

4.3 Lean production

Content C

- **Lean production:** when a firm tries to minimise the wastage of resources in its production process, for example, avoiding wasting time, effort, materials and money.
- **Just in Time (JIT) production:** a firm produces to order; it aims to have a zero level of stocks.
- **Continuous improvement:** when a firm improves its performance by making small improvements, on an ongoing basis, in many areas (also called "kaizen").
- **Simultaneous engineering:** when activities involved in product development are undertaken at the same time, rather than one after another, in order to save time.
- **Time management:** techniques managers use to reduce the time taken to complete a task, thereby increasing efficiency.

Analysis AN

- Just in time production can reduce the costs of holding stocks (for example, warehousing and security costs).
- Just in time production relies on the cooperation of suppliers (to make regular deliveries) and employees (to produce on time).
- Lean production can reduce a firm's costs and make it more competitive.
- Time management techniques can enable a firm to complete tasks more efficiently. For example, it may mean it can launch a product more quickly than its rivals, or respond more quickly to customer enquiries.
- Continuous improvement can improve quality and help cut costs.

Evaluation E

- Just in time production may not be appropriate if suppliers are not reliable or cannot deliver regularly.
- Just in time production may not be desirable if suppliers offer big discounts for large orders.
- Just in time production can cause problems if there are difficulties with supplies (for example, a fire at the suppliers), because there are no buffer stocks.
- Lean production improves efficiency, but the extent to which this provides a competitive advantage depends on what other firms are doing. If they are adopting the same techniques, the relative advantages may not be so great.
- Kaizen improves an existing system. If the system itself is not the right one to begin with (or is out of date), it may be better to make more radical changes.
- Not everyone will welcome kaizen. Employees may find it irritating and disruptive to keep changing the way they do things.

> ### Examiner's advice
> When answering exam questions on lean production:
> - Don't assume lean production is always a good thing. If the right conditions are not present (for example, reliable suppliers) it may lead to problems such as running out of stocks.

Lean production maths

Worked example 1

Using kaizen a firm making plastic buttons manages to reduce the unit costs per item by 0.1p. The present level of output is 200 000 units a week. How much is saved per week?

Assume the firm works a 46-week year and output levels are constant. How much would be saved per year?

Overall saving per week = 0.1 × 200 000 = 20 000 pence = £200 per week.

Overall saving per working year = £200 × 46 = £9200

This question illustrates that even a relatively small saving per item can add up to a significant overall reduction in a firm's costs.

Worked example 2

Using lean production techniques a firm reduces its stock levels by 4000 units. The stockholding costs were calculated to be £0.5 a unit and the rate of interest is 10% per annum in the bank.

a What are the savings in stockholding costs?

b What interest can be earned if this money is now invested in the bank for one year?

a Savings in stockholding costs = £0.5 × 4000 = £2000

b £2000 invested would earn $\dfrac{10}{100}$ × £2000 = £200 in one year

Practice questions

Maths questions

1 A firm's unit costs are 50 pence a unit. It produces 6000 units per day. Lean production techniques reduce the unit cost by 5%.
Calculate the savings per day as a result of lean production.

2 A firm holds 500 000 units of stock worth £4 each. The bank interest rate is 5% per annum.
Calculate the interest lost in one year through holding stocks rather than putting the money in the bank.

Diagram questions

1 Which of the diagrams below best represents a kaizen approach to improving productivity?

a

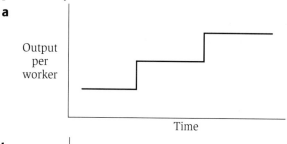

b

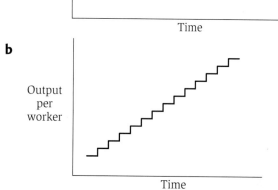

2 Tick the correct circles for a lean production system.

	High	Low
Stock levels	◯	◯
Number of orders of stocks	◯	◯
Amount ordered each time	◯	◯
Desired lead time	◯	◯
Flexibility	◯	◯
Waste levels	◯	◯
Number of deliveries of supplies	◯	◯

Quick questions

1 Just in time production:
   a Holds high levels of stock, just in case
   b Can only be used in job production
   c Produces items to order
   d Can only occur with mass production.

2 When developing a product, a firm may try to save time by undertaking the different activities involved at the same time. This is called s.....................
e..........................

3 Kaizen involves radical and quick change to an organisation. True or false?

4 An approach to production that attempts to reduce the wastage of time and resources is known as l....... production.

5 In JIT production, the buffer stocks are likely to be *low/high*.
Choose the correct option.

6 Continuous improvement relies on employees' ideas. It is most likely to require an *autocratic/democratic* approach to management
Choose the correct option.

7 Just in time production is most likely to be appropriate if:
   a Suppliers are unreliable
   b Relations with staff are poor
   c The stockholding costs are high.

8 Fast product development is most important when:
   a The product life cycle is very long.
   b The market is uncompetitive.
   c The pace of innovation is rapid.

9 Lean production does not usually involve:
   a self-checking
   b delegation
   c empowerment
   d high stocks

10 A firm is likely to hold more stocks if:
   a Lead time is low.
   b Suppliers are unreliable.
   c Usage rates are low.
   d The opportunity cost is high.

11 Kaizen needs high levels of capital investment. True or false?

12 A JIT system works best when the lead time is *high/low*.
Choose the correct option.

13 Under lean production, employees take more responsibility for their work.
Herzberg would classify this as a m..................

14 Under lean production, employees are involved in decision making. This can
help to fulfil the highest level of needs in Maslow's hierarchy, known as
s..............-a..........................

15 Under lean production, a great deal of attention is paid to employees because
they are so important in the process. According to the Hawthorne Works study,
by Elton ...., employees should respond positively to this attention.

What did you score?

Now check your answers, giving yourself one mark for each one correct.

If you scored:

12–15 **Congratulations! You clearly know these topics well. Now move on
to the next section.**

8–11 **This is quite a good score. It shows that you know some sections of
these topics. However, there are some areas you need to revise.
Why not look over the material again before moving on to the next
section?**

Less than 8 **This is less than half marks. You obviously need to revise these
topics again.**

Marking exam answers

Question

Discuss the possible advantages and disadvantages of introducing lean production into
a firm that produces computers in a highly competitive industry.

(10 marks)

Marked answer

Lean production is good because it means less stocks. **C** This means that it can be
cheaper for the firm. It does not have to have a warehouse and so it can sell this and
earn revenue. It also does not need to have staff to look after the stocks so this
reduces salaries. Costs are also reduced because stocks don't have to be looked after
and guarded and protected and so profits can increase. **AN**

But having no stocks can be dangerous because you can run out and this means you
cannot produce. **C** This means you cannot sell anything and so cannot earn money. **AN**

Overall, whether lean production is a good thing depends on whether you are going to
run out of stocks or not. If you think you will end up being unable to produce (for
example, because suppliers don't deliver) this is not a good move. **E**

> ### Examiner's comment
>
> This answer is rather narrow. Lean production involves all attempts to reduce
> wastage, not just reducing stock levels. Also, there is no reference to the computer
> industry. However, it deals with the stock issue well.
>
> **Mark: Content: 2/2 Application: 0/2 Analysis: 3/3 Evaluation: 2/3 Total: 7/10**

Your chance to mark

Mark the answer to this question, using the marking scheme on page xvii.

Question

Analyse the possible benefits to a leisure centre of adopting a kaizen approach.

(7 marks)

Student answer

Kaizen involves small changes to improve a firm's performance gradually over time. These can happen in all areas: the way members are greeted and shown round the centre, the way the centre is cleaned and checked to make sure it is safe, the way the duties are allocated and the tasks undertaken.

All in all kaizen can affect every aspect of the centre's operations. This can help to make this centre better than other leisure options. People have plenty of opportunities to decide what to do with their spare time. They can go to a leisure centre or they can go to the cinema or watch television. The better the centre is, the more likely people are to choose it. The other options (other centres) will be improving – if you don't improve, you will lose customers to them.

Mark: Content: _ /2 Application: _ /2 Analysis: _ /3 Total: _ /7

Now look at page 118 to compare your comments and marks with the examiner's.

5 External environment, objectives and strategy

5.1 Economic and competitive environment

Content

- **Capacity:** the maximum output a firm can produce with its existing resources.
- **Excess capacity:** when a firm could produce more output with its existing resources than it is actually producing.
- **Capacity shortage:** when a firm wants to produce more than it can with its existing resources.
- **Excess demand:** too much demand in the market compared to supply.
- **Excess supply:** the amount demanded by customers is less than the amount supplied by firms.
- **Rationalisation:** actions a firm takes to reduce its costs, for example by reducing capacity or making redundancies.
- **Subcontract:** when one firm produces on behalf of another. A firm may produce for another firm to increase its own capacity utilisation.
- **Unfair competition:** anti-competitive behaviour that acts against the public interest. Includes cartels (when firms work together to restrict prices), monopolies and predatory pricing (where one firm undercuts others to gain control of a market). In the UK, competitive behaviour is regulated by the Office of Fair Trading.
- **Monopoly:** one firm dominates a market. Under UK law, a monopoly is defined as a firm having more than 25% market share. In the UK, monopolies are regulated by the Competition Commission.
- **Macro-economics:** economic issues relating to the economy as a whole, for example inflation and exchange rates.
- **GDP:** gross domestic product. Measures the income of an economy over one year.
- **Recession:** a fall in national income (GDP).
- **Business cycle:** the pattern of GDP over time. Most economies go through a cycle of boom, slump, recession and recovery over time. Also called the trade cycle.
- **Interest rates:** the cost of borrowing money and the reward for saving. In the UK, interest rates are set by the Monetary Policy Committee.
- **Overheads:** costs that are not directly related to the production process. Also called indirect costs. For example, administration costs, senior managers' salaries.
- **Exchange rate:** measures the cost of one currency in terms of another.
- **Inflation:** a sustained increase in the general price level.
- **Deflation:** when prices are falling.
- **Retail Price Index (RPI):** a measure of inflation.
- **Structural unemployment:** when people are looking for work but cannot find a job because the structure of the economy has changed. For example, coal-miners may find it difficult to get work in the UK because the UK no longer has a competitive advantage in this sector so many coal mines have closed.
- **Cyclical unemployment:** when people are looking for work but cannot find a job because there is a lack of demand for goods and services throughout the economy.
- **Taxes:** charges imposed by the government and paid by households and firms. Direct taxes are paid out of income or profits; indirect taxes are placed on goods and services and paid when the items are bought (for example, taxes on petrol).

Analysis

- A firm's capacity is the maximum output it can produce. This can act as a constraint, limiting the amount it can sell.
- A firm's capacity may be higher than the level of demand, in which case the fixed costs per unit are likely to be high (because the fixed costs are spread over relatively few units).
- Changing capacity may be difficult and expensive. For example, the firm may have to build a new factory.
- If a firm has excess capacity it may:
  - ☐ cut prices or boost its promotional activities to try and increase demand
  - ☐ rationalise to reduce capacity
  - ☐ produce for other companies by subcontracting.
- If a firm has a capacity shortage it may:
  - ☐ increase prices to reduce demand
  - ☐ start a waiting list
  - ☐ increase capacity
  - ☐ subcontract to other producers to get the output produced.
- An increase in interest rates:
  - ☐ increases a firm's overheads (reducing profits)
  - ☐ increases demand for the currency (increasing the exchange rate)
  - ☐ makes it more expensive to borrow money (and so is likely to reduce demand for goods, especially those bought on credit).
- A strong currency means that a country's exports are more expensive in other currencies, which may reduce sales abroad. Also, the strong currency has more purchasing power abroad, which makes imports cheaper in terms of the domestic currency.
- Inflation may be caused by too much demand relative to supply (demand-pull inflation) or an increase in costs, such as higher wages (cost-push inflation).
- An increase in GDP may lead to an increase in demand (as consumers have more income).
- High levels of unemployment may mean lower levels of spending due to less income.
- The business cycle can make it difficult for firms to plan, because the levels of demand change over time.
- Demand-pull inflation is usually associated with shortages and queues. Firms may experience waiting lists and higher profit margins.
- Cost-push inflation may reduce profit margins if a firm does not want to, or cannot, pass on cost increases.
- Deflation is usually associated with falling levels of demand, or when there is too much supply in an industry.

Evaluation

- The decision about the appropriate level of capacity will depend on the costs, the availability of resources and the expected level of demand.
- The impact of a change in interest rates depends on the extent to which a firm has borrowed, the amount the interest rate goes up or down and how sensitive demand is to interest rates (for example, interest rate changes are more likely to affect demand for houses than for sandwiches).

- The impact of a change in exchange rates depends on the amount of the increase or decrease and the extent to which a firm trades abroad or buys items from abroad.

- The impact of a change in GDP depends on how income elastic demand is for a product. For example, demand for champagne is likely to be more sensitive to changes in income than demand for pencils.

- The impact of inflation on a firm depends on how high or low inflation is, the cause of inflation and how high inflation is compared to other countries.

- The ability to change capacity depends on the industry. In the chemicals industry it may require a new factory, so capacity suddenly jumps. In a college it may simply mean hiring a new teacher and finding a free room, so capacity can increase in smaller steps.

Examiner's advice

When answering exam questions on economic and competitive environment influences:

- Higher inflation does not necessarily mean that people cannot afford to buy products. It depends on what is happening to income as well.

- Higher inflation does not necessarily mean that demand will fall. The reason prices are going up may be because demand is so high.

- If you are asked a question about economic factors, be careful to stay focused on the actual topic you are asked about. For example, if you are asked about a recession, write about this. Don't wander off into other topics. If you write "In a recession a government may lower interest to boost the economy. Lower interest rates mean it is cheaper to borrow and so …" you are now writing about interest rates, not the recession.

- Remember that firms buy and sell in many different markets. Just because the UK market is in recession does not necessarily mean that demand for a UK firm is falling – it may be selling overseas.

- Try to relate changes in the external environment to the internal functions of the business (marketing, finance, operations and human resource management).

Economic influences maths

- **National income changes**

  $$\text{Percentage change in GDP} = \frac{\text{Change in value}}{\text{Original value}} \times 100$$

	GDP
Year 1	£500bn
Year 2	£600bn

  For the data above:

  $$\text{Percentage change in GDP} = \frac{600 - 500}{500} \times 100 = \frac{100}{500} \times 100 = 20\%$$

- **Index numbers**

  Index numbers show the percentage change in value of a variable (such as national income or prices) compared to a previous point known as the "base". The base always has value 100.

  Simply looking at the difference between the given index number and the base of 100 automatically gives the percentage change. For example, if the variable now has a value of 105 this is a difference of 5% $\left(\frac{105 - 100}{100} \times 100\right)$. A price index number of 146 means that the price is 46% higher than the base point.

Worked example 1

		National income index
Year	1 (the base year)	100
Year	2	110
Year	3	120
Year	4	95

The above figures show us that:

☐ In Year 2 income is 10% higher than Year 1 (because the index number has increased by 10).

☐ In Year 3 income is 20% higher than Year 1 (because the index number has increased by 20).

☐ In Year 4 income is 5% less than in Year 1 (because the index number has decreased by 5).

To calculate the change between Year 2 and Year 3, calculate:

$$\frac{\text{Change}}{\text{Original value}} \times 100$$

$$\frac{120 - 110}{110} \times 100 = 9.1\%$$

Index numbers can be used to show percentage changes in anything, for example sales, profits, costs or wages.

For example, if the index number for wages is 127 (with a base in 2002 of 100), this means that wages have increased 27% since 2002. Note that these figures do not actually show the value of the numbers (we do not know how much wages are). They simply show how much the variable has *changed*.

Worked example 2

	GDP growth
1999	3%
2000	2%
2001	1%
2002	−0.5%

Between 1999 and 2001 GDP is still growing: what has happened is that it is growing at a slower rate. Many candidates, faced with such figures, would say that GDP has fallen. Don't make this mistake!

GDP *has* fallen in 2002, when the growth rate is negative.

Practice questions

 Maths questions

1

	National income
Year 1	£500bn
Year 2	£475bn
Year 3	£450bn

a Calculate the percentage change in national income

  i from Year 1 to Year 2

  ii from Year 2 to Year 3.

b What stage of the business cycle is the economy in during these three years? Explain your answer.

2

	Price index
Year 1	100
Year 2	105
Year 3	107

a What was the rate of inflation from Year 1 to Year 3?

b What was the rate of inflation from Year 2 to Year 3?

Diagram questions

1

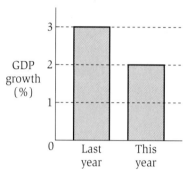

Which statement best describes the situation shown in the diagram?

a National income is falling at a fast rate

b National income is falling at a slow rate

c National income is rising at a fast rate

d National income is rising at a slow rate

2 Label the four main stages of the business cycle on the diagram below.

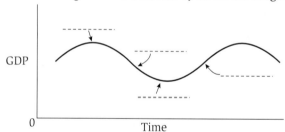

3

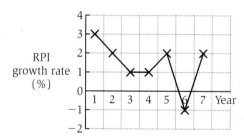

a What happened to prices in years 1 to 3?

b In which year did the economy first experience deflation?

Quick questions

1 Which one of the following is an example of unfair competition?

a Increasing your spending on advertising

b Developing a new product

c Cutting the price below costs so competitors cannot compete and have to close down

d Having a summer sale

2 If the exchange rate changes from £1 : $1.65 to £1 : $1.70, has the pound appreciated or depreciated?

3 Many economies go through the stages of boom, recession, slump and recovery. This is known as the ....

4 Excess capacity occurs when:

 a Demand for a firm's products is higher than its capacity

 b There is 100% capacity utilisation

 c There is over-utilisation of capacity

 d A firm is able to supply more than is demanded.

5 When there is high unemployment in the economy, the level of spending is likely to be *high/low*. Choose the correct option.

6 The biggest sector of the UK economy in terms of employment generated is the *primary/secondary/tertiary* sector. Choose the correct option.

7 If unemployment increases as a result of a fall in demand throughout the economy for goods and services, this is known as .... unemployment.

8 In a recession national income:

 a Increases at a slower rate

 b Falls

 c Increases at a higher rate

 d Stays constant

9 The initials GDP stand for G.............. D................ P..........

10 If the general level of prices is falling this is known as ....

11 If interest rates increase:

 a The exchange rate is likely to increase in value

 b The exchange rate is likely to fall in value

 c Savings are likely to fall

 d Firms are likely to borrow more

12 Inflation has decreased from 5% to 3%. This means:

 a Prices in general have fallen

 b All prices have fallen

 c Prices are increasing at a slower rate

 d Prices are decreasing more slowly

13 Inflation is usually measured by the R........ P........ I..........

14 A depreciating exchange rate is most likely to benefit *importers/exporters*. Choose the correct option. Explain your answer.

15 Interest rates in the UK are controlled by:

 a The Home Office

 b The Monetary Policy Committee

 c Local councils

 d The Balance of Payments

What did you score?

Now check your answers, giving yourself one mark for each one correct.

If you scored:

12–15   **Congratulations! You clearly know these topics well. Now move on to the next section.**

8–11   **This is quite a good score. It shows that you know some sections of these topics. However, there are some areas you need to revise. Why not look over the material again before moving on to the next section?**

Less than 8   **This is less than half marks. You obviously need to revise these topics again.**

Marking exam answers

Question

Examine the ways in which a football club might react in a recession. **(7 marks)**

Marked answer

A recession means that the economy is collapsing. This means people have no money and spend less. **C** This means there is no demand and so nothing is bought. This means the football club will go out of business because no one can afford to go to see the team play. **AP** This means jobs will be lost and this means the economy will go even further into recession which is bad for the economy. This is a vicious circle which just gets worse.

> ## Examiner's comment
>
> The candidate has some understanding of a recession but the answer is too definite and too extreme. It is not true that there will be "no demand" or that "nothing is bought" or that "no one can afford to see the team play". Whilst demand may be affected, it is a question of degree.
>
> The answer does refer to a football club but there is only a limited attempt to relate to this type of business. Furthermore the candidate does not actually focus on how the football club might react. Instead he or she concentrates on the impact of a recession, rather than what a firm might do.
>
> **Mark: Content: 1/2   Application: 1/2   Analysis: 0/3   Total: 2/7**

Your chance to mark

Mark the answer to this question, using the marking scheme on page xvii.

Question

To what extent is a change in interest rates likely to affect the success of a company that produces toiletries such as shampoos and soaps? **(10 marks)**

Student answer

Interest rates are the cost of borrowing money and the reward for saving. If interest rates are low it is cheap to borrow and the reward for saving is low. This is likely to encourage more borrowing and less saving. This may encourage demand for products and so sales may increase.

This is most likely to affect products that are bought on credit or with borrowing, such as cars and houses. It is less likely to affect products which do not cost very much to begin with and which you do not need to borrow to buy. In the case of toiletries, for example, most of these are relatively cheap and so demand may not be affected very much. However there may be some shift in terms of the types of toiletries bought. With low interest rates, customers may have less to pay on their mortgage and so feel they can spend more on luxury toiletries. They may move upmarket in terms of the brands purchased or products bought (for example, foam bath as well as or instead of soap).

The effect will depend on the extent to which interest rates have changed (if they have not changed a lot the effect will probably be small), which way they have changed (for example, higher rates reduce the income most people have because they have more to pay on their borrowing and most people are borrowers) and how long they change for (if it is just a day or two it may not have much effect).

Mark: Content: _/2   Application: _/2   Analysis: _/3   Evaluation: _/3   Total: _/10

Now look at page 119 to compare your comments and marks with the examiner's.

5.2 Political, social and technological environment

Content

- **Consumer laws:** legislation intended to protect consumers, for example to protect them from being sold goods that are not accurately described. Consumer laws include the Sale of Goods Act, the Trades Description Act and the Weights and Measures Act.
- **Competition laws:** legislation that regulates the way in which firms compete. For example, monopolies may be investigated by the Competition Commission and firms may be fined (up to 10% of turnover) for anti-competitive behaviour such as cartels. Competition Acts were passed in 1980 and 1988.
- **Employment laws:** legislation to protect employees at work, for example guaranteeing a minimum wage, or protection from discrimination. Employment laws include the Race Relations Act and the Sex Discrimination Act.
- **Health and safety laws:** legislation to provide safe and healthy working conditions. Under the Health and Safety Act 1974, employers have to "ensure as far as is reasonably practicable the health, safety and welfare at work" of their employees.
- **Social responsibility:** obligations to society that a firm might decide to accept.
- **Business ethics:** decisions concerning the rights and wrongs of business actions.
- **Stakeholders:** individuals, groups or organisations that affect and are affected by a firm's activities, for example shareholders, customers, employees, creditors, suppliers, local community, the government.

Analysis

- Under UK competition law, monopolies (firms with a market share of more than 25%) may be investigated by the Competition Commission. Monopolies are not assumed to be undesirable. An investigation into a firm is to decide whether the firm is acting against the public interest. If it is not, no action is taken. If the monopoly is acting against the public interest, the firm may be forced to sell off brands or part of the business, or reduce its prices. The Competition Commission may also prevent mergers going ahead if they create a monopoly that would act against the public interest.
- Under UK employment law:
  - ☐ Firms cannot discriminate on the basis of gender, race or ethnic origin.
  - ☐ Employees who have been employed by a firm for more than two years must receive notice and compensation if they are made redundant.
  - ☐ Employees are entitled to a minimum wage.
- Under the Health and Safety Act 1974, firms must provide the necessary safety equipment and clothing for employees free, have a written safety policy (if a firm has five or more employees) and provide a safe working environment. The Health and Safety Executive implements the Act.
- Under UK Consumer Law, goods sold must be "as described", "fit for purpose" and "of a satisfactory quality".
- Laws may restrict a firm's behaviour by preventing certain activities, for example advertising cigarettes. This may result in a loss in business. A change in the law may also increase costs. For example, safety laws may mean a change to the way goods are produced, which could be expensive to implement.

- Laws may create new opportunities for firms, for example by creating new trade opportunities such as the European Union.
- Laws may protect firms from other organisations, for example from unfair competition.
- By behaving in a socially responsible manner, a firm may attract more investors, more staff and more customers. However, it may also increase costs (for example, changes to the product or the packaging or the process) and prevent the firm engaging in profitable activities (for example, selling weapons).
- Any decision may involve a conflict of ethics. For example, closing a UK factory and producing overseas may mean UK employees lose their jobs but may be essential to keep the business going.
- Meeting the needs of one stakeholder group may be at the expense of another group. For example, improving employees' working conditions may reduce shareholders' profits. However, meeting the needs of one group may benefit another group as well. For example, improving employees' working conditions may lead to higher morale and better profits in the long term.
- Technology may improve products and processes (what is produced and how it is produced).
- Technology may cut costs (for example, through more efficient processes) and increase revenue (for example, by adding value and differentiating so a higher price can be charged).

Evaluation **E**

- The benefits of socially responsible behaviour depend on the attitude of consumers, employees and investors – to what extent do they care about this type of behaviour?
- What is and what is not ethical may depend on your perspective. The decision to relocate overseas may be seen as ethical because it maintains profits and rewards for the owners, but may be seen as unethical because it loses UK jobs.
- Behaving ethically may reduce profits because it may involve higher costs (for example, paying employees more than you have to). However, ethical policies may increase profits by attracting more demand (for example, The Body Shop).
- The power of a stakeholder group depends on its resources, how well organised it is and its impact on business behaviour.
- You cannot say "the law is good for business" or the "law is bad for business"– it depends which law you are referring to.
- Laws do not stay static; they change over time. For example, in recent years the competition law has introduced heavy fines for firms who behave uncompetitively.
- There is much greater interest in what firms do for their stakeholder groups than there used to be in the past. Firms are subject to much more scrutiny now in this area.
- The impact of technology depends on whether you are the firm adopting it or whether others have adopted it and you have not.
- The introduction of new technology may be resisted because staff worry about:
  - ☐ their ability to use it
  - ☐ their jobs
  - ☐ their existing skills becoming out of date.
- Technology can provide a competitive advantage by enabling a firm to lower its prices, or enabling it to react more quickly to change (for example, launching new products more rapidly). It may also give a product new features, so the firm can charge higher prices.

Examiner's advice

When answering exam questions on political, social and technological influences:

- Remember that new technology does not always lead to unemployment – it also creates markets and jobs. Think of DVDs and computer software.
- Remember that not everyone is interested in social and environmental issues. A firm that behaves socially responsibly may attract more investors or customers, but it depends on how much customers really care and how much they know about the firm's behaviour. Some companies are very high profile when it comes to their social behaviour (for example, The Body Shop) but do you know much about the behaviour of the firm that makes the pens you buy? Or the one that manufactures the CDs you buy?
- Remember that there are major differences in the political and legal environment in different countries, for example how much the government intervenes in the economy, the amount of legal protection for employees.

Practice questions

 Diagram questions

1   Various business issues are listed below. Identify which type of law would cover each issue. Write each issue in the correct section of the table.

   a   Ensuring customers are sold goods in a suitable condition.
   b   Ensuring reasonable steps are taken to keep the workplace safe.
   c   Preventing a firm abusing its monopoly power.
   d   Ensuring staff are properly trained to use machinery.
   e   Preventing firms misrepresenting their goods to their customers.
   f   Preventing firms forming cartels and acting against the public interest.

Consumer law	Competition law	Health and Safety law

2   On the diagram below, identify four stakeholder groups of a school or college:

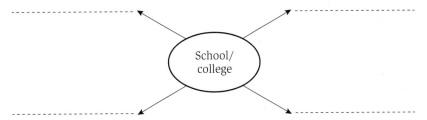

3   Match each aim with the most likely stakeholder group. Write them in the correct section of the table.

   a   Job security
   b   Higher dividends
   c   Investment in local facilities
   d   Good value for money

Stakeholder group	Objective
Shareholders	
Employees	
Customers	
Local community	

4 Tick the correct circles.

	True	False
The Trade Descriptions Act is an employment law.	◯	◯
A shareholder is a stakeholder of the business.	◯	◯
Monopolies are illegal in the UK.	◯	◯
The UK has a minimum wage.	◯	◯
A monopoly must have 100% market share.	◯	◯
Companies are owned by all their stakeholders.	◯	◯
You have the right to insist a shop sells an item at the same price as its competitors.	◯	◯

Quick questions

1 Consumer law does *not* include:
  a The rights of buyers
  b Information provided by sellers
  c The way goods are described
  d Minimum wage legislation

2 Improvements in technology always lead to job losses. True or false?

3 Which of the following issues is not covered by employment law?
  a Discrimination against staff
  b The number of hours worked in a week
  c The prices of goods sold
  d The contract given to employees

4 In the UK, firms that are found to have behaved in an anti-competitive way may be fined:
  a A maximum of £100 000
  b A minimum of £1000
  c Up to 1% of profits
  d Up to 10% of turnover

5 Which one of the following statements is true?
  a Ethical firms are always more profitable than unethical ones.
  b Ethical firms are always less profitable than unethical ones.
  c Ethics concern what is right or wrong.
  d What is ethical is always determined by the law.

6 Which one of the following statements is true?
  a A shareholder is not a stakeholder.
  b A stakeholder is always a shareholder.
  c A shareholder is a stakeholder.
  d All stakeholders have a vote in a company's actions.

7 Under UK competition law, monopolies are illegal. True or false?

8 When firms act together to set prices and output this is known as a c............

9 Under UK consumer law:
  a Customers can insist that a firm matches the prices of its competitors.
  b The goods sold in a shop must be "as described".
  c Consumers have the right to a 10% discount on Saturdays.
  d The goods sold must be "of exceptional quality".

10   Under UK consumer law, the goods sold in a shop must be:
   a   "of satisfactory quality"
   b   "free at the point of purchase"
   c   "the same price in all of a firm's shops"
   d   "of the highest quality possible"

11   Under UK employment law:
   a   A firm cannot make staff redundant.
   b   A firm cannot discriminate on the basis of an employee's ethnic origin.
   c   A firm must hire equal numbers of men and women.
   d   A firm cannot pay staff more without government permission.

12   Under the Health and Safety Act firms must provide a healthy and safe working environment:
   a   "no matter what the cost"
   b   "as far as is reasonably practicable"
   c   "providing it is not too expensive"
   d   "providing it does not damage the firm's competitiveness"

13   Which of the following is *not* a consumer law?
   a   Sale of Goods Act
   b   Sex Discrimination Act
   c   Trades Description Act

14   Which of the following is *not* an employment law?
   a   Race Relations Act
   b   Redundancy Payments Act
   c   Weights and Measures Act

15   In the UK, monopolies can be investigated by the C.................. Commission.

What did you score?
Now check your answers, giving yourself one mark for each one correct.
If you scored:

12–15   **Congratulations! You clearly know these topics well. Now move on to the next section.**

8–11   **This is quite a good score. It shows that you know some sections of these topics. However, there are some areas you need to revise. Why not look over the material again before moving on to the next section?**

Less than 8 **This is less than half marks. You obviously need to revise these topics again.**

Marking exam answers

Question

Analyse the ways in which the law might affect the success of a café.   **(7 marks)**

Marked answer

The law affects many aspects of business and the café will be affected in all kinds of ways. For example, the way that food is prepared and served will be closely controlled with many regulations. **C** **AP** This will determine exactly how things are done (and will be inspected) and may increase costs as different types of food will need to be stored in particular ways. **AP** **AN**

The law will also affect the way staff are treated. **C** For example, waiters must be paid the minimum wage and this could increase costs. **AP** **AN** Employees must receive proper training in anything involving health and safety and if they have worked there long enough they will also have rights regarding redundancy; this could make getting rid of people more difficult and more expensive. **AN**

Overall, legislation will affect what is done and how it is done. **C** In some ways this might make succeeding more difficult, but if all cafés have to do the same it is not so bad. **AN**

Examiner's comment

A very good answer which shows a solid command of the topic. The arguments cover several different areas from staff to health and safety and highlight the possible consequences for a café. The end part is very good, recognising that the negative impact of legislation is not so bad if all cafés are affected.

Mark: Content: 2/2   Application: 2/2   Analysis: 3/3   Total: 7/7

Your chance to mark

Mark the answer to this question, using the marking scheme on page xvii.

Question

Discuss whether behaving ethically inevitably reduces a manufacturer's profits.

(11 marks)

Student answer

A firm that is not ethical will be closed down because no one will buy from you. These days everyone has ethics and so if you don't you will not sell. People don't want to buy from firms that do not have proper ethics and they cannot survive. Businesses should lead the way and show how to behave. That way we admire them and buy from them and want to work for them, so they make better profits. If they don't do this they are bad and no one wants to be associated with them and profits fall. You won't make money by not being liked. It is much better to be popular by doing what is regarded as the right thing. Being ethical should appeal to customers and make it easier to get good employees.

Mark: Content: _ /2 Application: _ /2 Analysis: _ /3 Evaluation: _ /3 Total: _ /10

Now look at page 119 to compare your comments and marks with the examiner's.

5.3 Start ups and objectives

Content

- **Patent:** legal protection for an innovative product or process.
- **Copyright:** legal protection for written and for formal work such as a book, play or song.
- **Sole trader:** an individual who sets up his or her own business.
- **Partnership:** a form of business where individuals join together in pursuit of profit. Partnerships usually involve between 2 and 20 people and partners share the rewards of the business. Partnerships are common in the legal, accounting and medical professions, where individuals share their knowledge, expertise and resources.
- **Company:** an organisation that has a separate legal existence from its owners. It can sue and be sued. It is owned by its shareholders.
- **Private limited company:** a company that is owned by shareholders but the shares cannot be advertised or traded on the Stock Exchange. A private limited company has "ltd" after its name.
- **Public limited company:** a company that is owned by shareholders and the shares can be advertised and traded on the Stock Exchange. A public limited company has "plc" after its name.
- **Limited liability:** when the investors in an organisation can lose the amount they invested but no more – they cannot lose their personal possessions.
- **Unlimited liability:** when there is no limit to investors' liability. For example, their personal possessions may be claimed if the firm is liquidated.
- **Divorce of ownership and control:** when the people who control an organisation (managers) are not the same people who own the business (the shareholders).
- **Directors:** individuals elected by shareholders to represent their interests and watch over the managers.
- **Corporate aim:** an organisation's overall goal.
- **Objectives:** quantifiable targets, such as a 50% increase in sales in three years.
- **Business plan:** sets out the firm's objectives and strategy, including marketing plans, cash-flow forecast, profit and loss forecasts, production plans.
- **SWOT analysis:** an examination of the Strengths and Weaknesses of a firm as well as the Opportunities and Threats it faces.
- **Primary sector:** the first stage of the production process, for example farming, oil exploration, fishing (extractive industries).
- **Secondary sector:** firms involved in manufacturing, for example car production.
- **Tertiary sector:** the service sector, for example restaurants.
- The **public sector** refers to organisations owned by the government (for example, the National Health Service). The **private sector** refers to organisations owned by private individuals (for example, sole traders and companies).
- **Privatisation:** the transfer of an organisation from the public sector to the private sector.
- **Nationalisation:** the transfer of an organisation from the private sector to the public sector.

Analysis

- An inventor can protect his or her idea with a patent so that competitors cannot easily imitate the product. This means that the inventor may be able to offer something unique, which customers may be willing to pay more for.

- Without limited liability companies would find it much more difficult to attract investors, because investors would be worried about losing their personal possessions.

- Objectives can help to communicate what senior management is trying to achieve. They can motivate staff and be used to review progress.

- The divorce between ownership and control can mean that managers are pursuing their own interests instead of the owners' interests.

- SWOT analysis is an important part of strategic planning. Firms must consider where they are at the moment, and what the future opportunities and threats are, before deciding on their strategy.

- Strengths and weaknesses concern the internal aspects of the firm at the moment, for example a strong brand name or poor management.

- Opportunities and threats concern future external change, for example. a new market opening up or new firms entering the market.

- A private limited company can control the sales of its shares. Also, it does not have to reveal as much information in its published accounts as a public limited company.

- You cannot restrict who the shares in a plc are sold to. This means that a company may be the victim of a hostile takeover.

- A business plan can be useful to show to potential investors, to convince them this is a good investment. It can also help managers decide on what they should be doing and monitor their progress.

- Sole traders can set up in business relatively easily and have the advantage of making decisions for themselves (and keeping the profits). However, sole traders have unlimited liability, may lack managerial expertise in some areas and may have limited sources of finance.

- A partnership is likely to have more input in terms of ideas and finance than a sole trader. Until recently, partners could only have limited liability if they did not take part in the day-to-day decisions of the business (these people were called "sleeping partners"). At least one partner had to have unlimited liability.

  Under the 2000 Limited Liability Partnership Act, a partnership can now have its own legal status separate from its owners (just like a company). Also partners (now called members) in the business can have limited liability.

- The production process varies in the primary, secondary and tertiary sectors. For example, manufacturing usually has stock levels, whereas the tertiary sector does not. In manufacturing the production process often happens away from the customer and the product is sold through intermediaries, such as retailers. In services, production often happens directly with the customer (e.g. teaching).

Evaluation **E**

- The value of objectives depends on how they are introduced. If objectives are simply imposed on subordinates, people may resent it. It also depends on how realistic the targets are – if they are unrealistic they may not motivate people.

- The right type of organisation for a business (sole trader or company) depends on a range of issues, such as:
  - ☐ how far an individual wants to remain in control,
  - ☐ the willingness of the owners to publish financial information about the business,
  - ☐ the need to raise finance from selling shares.

- The value of a SWOT analysis depends on whether the managers identify relevant factors, whether they draw the right conclusions and whether they then implement the plan effectively.

Examiner's advice

When answering exam questions on start ups and objectives:

- Make sure that you know the advantages and disadvantages of different forms of business organisation (for example, sole trader versus private limited versus public limited company), because you are often asked to discuss what you think would be the best form for a particular business.
- Think about the problems and challenges of starting up a business. How would you do it? What would you want to know? What difficulties do you think you would have? You will often be given a case study about a start up and asked to evaluate how well the people involved managed the start up of their business.
- Make sure that you are clear of the differences between Strengths, Weaknesses, Opportunities and Threats. Sometimes students get these confused and list a weakness as a threat, or a strength as an opportunity.

Practice questions

Diagram questions

1 Different types of organisation are listed below. Write them under the correct headings in the table.

 a Printing company
 b Gas exploration company
 c Hotel
 d Oil company
 e Producer of consumer electronics goods
 f Tree-felling and timber business
 g Accountant
 h Lawyer
 i Computer manufacturer

Primary	Secondary	Tertiary

2 Four features of different business structures are given below.
 Write each one under the appropriate heading in the table.

 a Unlimited liability
 b Owned by shareholders
 c Has a separate legal identity from its owners
 d Does not have shares

Sole trader	Company

3 Write these three company roles in the correct boxes.
- ☐ Managers
- ☐ Shareholders
- ☐ Board of Directors

┌─────────────────────────────────────┐
│ .... │
│ The owners of a company.   │
└─────────────────────────────────────┘
                    ↓
┌─────────────────────────────────────┐
│ .... │
│ Elected by the owners.   │
└─────────────────────────────────────┘
                    ↓
┌─────────────────────────────────────┐
│ .... │
│ Control the company on a day-to-day basis. │
└─────────────────────────────────────┘

4 Which of these features relate to private limited companies and which relate to public limited companies? Write them in the correct sections of the table.
- **a** Shares can be sold on the Stock Exchange.
- **b** Has "ltd" after its name.
- **c** Cannot advertise its shares for sale.
- **d** Can place restrictions on the sale of shares.
- **e** Has "plc" after its name.
- **f** Cannot place restrictions on the sale of shares.

Private limited company	Public limited company

5 For each business feature given below, decide whether it is a strength, weakness, opportunity or threat. Write each feature in the correct section of the table.
- **a** High unit costs
- **b** Launch new product
- **c** Strong brand name
- **d** Recession

SWOT	Feature
Strength	
Weakness	
Opportunity	
Threat	

6 For each business factor given below, decide whether it is a strength, weakness, opportunity or threat. Write each factor in the correct section of the table.

   a The possibility of new entrants into the market

   b Poor cash flow

   c The possibility of a new niche market opening overseas

   d A well known brand name

SWOT	Feature
Strength	
Weakness	
Opportunity	
Threat	

Quick questions

1 A public limited company:

   a Must be bigger than a private limited company

   b Has unlimited liability

   c Has Ltd after its name

   d Is owned by its shareholders

2 Which one of the following statements is true?

   a A shareholder is a stakeholder.

   b A stakeholder must be a shareholder.

   c A shareholder is always employed by the company.

   d A shareholder is always a customer.

3 A business plan:

   a Is backward looking

   b Must be produced by companies by law

   c Is likely to contain a sales forecast

   d Guarantees a firm's success

4 a Kathy Tan has written a brilliant song that she is sure will be Number 1 one day. Her song is automatically protected by ....

   b Bob Holdness has an innovative idea for glass production. To protect his idea he could apply for a ....

5 A sole trader:

   a Is owned by shareholders

   b Has unlimited liability

   c Has limited liability

   d Is owned by the government

6 A television manufacturer is in the *primary/secondary/tertiary* sector. Choose the correct option.

7 A farm is part of the *primary/secondary/tertiary* sector of the economy. Choose the correct option.

8 Employees, investors, customers and the local community all have an interest in the activities of a business. This means they are all s....................

9 Which one of the following is *not* a strength of a firm?

   a Positive cash flow

   b A boom in the economy

   c Good management

   d Widespread distribution channels

10 Which one of the following is *not* a weakness of a firm?
  a Limited managerial expertise
  b A capacity shortage
  c More competition due to enter the market
  d Demotivated staff

11 Which one of the following represents an opportunity for a firm?
  a New entrants into the market
  b An adverse variance
  c Diseconomies of scale
  d Overseas expansion

12 Which one of the following represents a threat for a firm?
  a A decline in market growth
  b Economies of scale
  c Low unit costs
  d Favourable variance

13 Which one of the following is an example of a tertiary business?
  a A brewery
  b A farm
  c A steel company
  d A private school

14 The public sector refers to organisations owned by the general public. True or false?

15 When organisations are transferred from the public sector to the private sector, this is known as ....

What did you score?
Now check your answers, giving yourself one mark for each one correct.
If you scored:

12–15   **Congratulations! You clearly know these topics well. Now move on to the next section.**

8–11   **This is quite a good score. It shows that you know some sections of these topics. However, there are some areas you need to revise. Why not look over the material again before moving on to the next section?**

Less than 8 **This is less than half marks. You obviously need to revise these topics again.**

Marking exam answers

Question

Some of the present owners of a well established family printing business, which is a private limited company, are thinking of turning the business into a public limited company. Discuss the factors that might influence this decision.   **(10 marks)**

Marked answer

A private limited company is a ltd. A public limited company is a plc. **C**
The advantages of becoming a plc include:

■ More impressive to customers
■ Able to sell shares to the general public more easily
■ Shares can be quoted on the Stock Exchange and listed in the newspapers. **C**

The disadvantages are:

- Costs money to produce the documents to become a plc, for example legal fees
- Have to make more information available to the general public
- Cannot control sale of shares and so more vulnerable to takeover, because competitors may buy the shares and gain control. **C** **AN**

Examiner's comment

A rather basic answer that demonstrates an understanding of the topic areas but does not develop the points or try to place them in context. There is no reference at all to the fact that this is a family business or the fact that only some of the present owners seem to want to turn the business into a plc.

A better answer might have considered the loss of control, the willingness of the family of a "well established" business to give up part ownership and a consideration of why this was occurring.

The candidate has used a bullet point approach. This is not advisable, because it tends to prevent candidates from developing their points. For this type of question it is important to analyse – to do this you need a chain of argument, not just a list of points.

Mark: Content: 2/2 Application: 0/2 Analysis: 1/3 Evaluation: 0/3 Total: 3/10

Your chance to mark

Mark the answer to this question, using the marking scheme on page xvii.

Question

Gheeta Bandari is hoping to open her first business: a bakery. She has produced a business plan to show to the bank manager. To what extent will a business plan guarantee the success of her business? **(10 marks)**

Student answer

A business plan sets out the direction of the firm. This can help to coordinate actions and make sure the different areas of the business are aligned. A plan will be motivating by setting realistic targets and will also enable the managers to review their progress to see how far they have come relative to where they hoped to be. Reviewing such progress can in itself be useful since it provides more insights into the nature of the business and its environment.

However, a plan is just that – it still has to be implemented. Many plans come unstuck when you try to make them happen. People resist, things don't happen in the way you expected or when you expected them and external factors such as competitors' actions intervene.

Overall, a plan can help success but cannot guarantee it. It has to be executed properly and even then it relies on the fact that the plan is right. Not all plans are correct. As this is Gheeta's first business, she may not know much about the industry and so all her estimates may be inaccurate. A bad plan may be of limited use.

Mark: Content: _/2 Application: _/2 Analysis: _/3 Evaluation: _/3 Total: _/10

Now look at page 120 to compare your comments and marks with the examiner's.

Once you have worked your way through the rest of the book, use these tests to check whether you need to go over any areas again. The test questions cover all the different parts of the specification.

Test 1

1 What is meant by "market share"?
2 State four stages in the product life cycle.
3 State two internal sources of finance.
4 What is meant by a "debenture"?
5 What is meant by "delegation"?
6 When a manager tells staff what to do, this is known as an a...................... leadership style.
7 State five needs in Maslow's Hierarchy of Needs, starting with the lowest.
8 Diseconomies of scale occur when .... costs increase with an increase in the scale of operations.
9 The maximum output a firm can produce at any moment is called its ....
10 State four stages of the business cycle.
11 The RPI is used to measure inflation. The initials RPI stand for R...................... P...................... I......................
12 Investors in companies can only lose their investment and not any other savings because of L...................... L......................
13 Unemployment caused by a lack of demand in the economy is called .... unemployment.
14 Legal protection for a new product or process is known as a p......................
15 In SWOT analysis the initials stand for S...................... W...................... O...................... T......................

What did you score?
Now check your answers, giving yourself one mark for each one correct.
If you scored:

12–15 marks	This is a good score and suggests you know all the different areas of the specification quite well. Congratulations! You need to look at any questions you got wrong, just to fill in any gaps, but you seem to know the material well.
8–11 marks	This is quite a good score and suggests you have a good grasp of many areas of the specification. However there are obviously still some gaps. Look over the questions you got wrong and work through those units again.
4–7 marks	This is rather a weak score. Look at the questions you got wrong to identify the areas you need to work through again, then work through those units a second time.
Less than 4 marks	This is obviously a disappointing score. Work your way through this book again and then have another go.

Test 2

1   Market research that collects data for the first time is called p...................... research.

2   State the equation for the price elasticity of demand.

3   If managers assume that employees do not like work, this is an example of McGregor's Theory ....

4   Which theorist is associated with Scientific Management?

5   The minimum stock a firm wants to hold at any moment is called the b...................... stock.

6   Continuous production, when an item moves directly from one stage of the process to the next, is known as .... production.

7   The cost of borrowing money is called the ....

8   The price of one currency in terms of another is called the ....

9   Groups that affect and are affected by a firm's activities are called .... groups.

10   What is meant by "favourable variance"?

11   What is meant by the "span of control"?

12   Estimating the future demand and supply of labour is known as w...................... p......................

13   When a firm produces to order and does not hold stocks, this is known as .... in .... production.

14   Decisions about what organisations believe is right and wrong are known as business e......................

15   If there is a continuous increase in the general price level, this is known as i......................

What did you score?
Now check your answers, giving yourself one mark for each one correct.
If you scored:

12–15 marks	**This is a good score and suggests you know all the different areas of the specification quite well. Congratulations! You need to look at any questions you got wrong, just to fill in any gaps, but you seem to know the material well.**
8–11 marks	**This is quite a good score and suggests you have a good grasp of many areas of the specification. However there are obviously still some gaps. Look over the questions you got wrong and work through those units again.**
4–7 marks	**This is rather a weak score. Look at the questions you got wrong to identify the areas you need to work through again, then work through those units a second time.**
Less than 4 marks	**This is obviously a disappointing score. Work your way through this book again and then have another go.**

Test 3

1. A 95% confidence level means there is a 95% chance that a new product will succeed. True or false?
2. What does it mean if a product is described as "income elastic"?
3. What is meant by the term "break-even"?
4. State two external sources of finance.
5. What is meant by an "adverse variance"?
6. What is consultation?
7. When a manager asks staff what to do this is known as a d...................... leadership style.
8. If managers assume that employees want to work, this is an example of McGregor's Theory ....
9. A fall in unit cost associated with a larger scale of operations is known as .... of ....
10. The amount a firm is producing now as a proportion of its maximum output, is known as its c...................... u......................
11. When groups of items move together from one stage of a process to another, this is called .... production.
12. Money tied up in stocks could be invested elsewhere and therefore involves an o...................... cost.
13. A process of continuous gradual improvement is known as k......................
14. If a firm can produce more than is being demanded it has e...................... capacity.
15. What is meant by simultaneous engineering?

What did you score?

Now check your answers, giving yourself one mark for each one correct.

If you scored:

12–15 marks	This is a good score and suggests you know all the different areas of the specification quite well. Congratulations! You need to look at any questions you got wrong, just to fill in any gaps, but you seem to know the material well.
8–11 marks	This is quite a good score and suggests you have a good grasp of many areas of the specification. However there are obviously still some gaps. Look over the questions you got wrong and work through those units again.
4–7 marks	This is rather a weak score. Look at the questions you got wrong to identify the areas you need to work through again, then work through those units a second time.
Less than 4 marks	This is obviously a disappointing score. Work your way through this book again and then have another go.

Test 4

1 If prices in an economy are falling this is known as d......................

2 What is meant by the term "working capital"?

3 Herzberg identified two types of rewards for employees – those that prevent dissatisfaction and those that motivate. He called these two groups, "......................" factors and "......................" factors.

4 If a firm cannot produce enough to meet demand it has a capacity s......................

5 A private limited company has unlimited liability. True or false?

6 An objective is a long-term plan. True or false?

7 The time it takes between ordering supplies and them arriving is called .... time.

8 The process of identifying how the best in the world undertake an activity and trying to learn from this is called b......................

9 An approach to production which attempts to minimise waste is known as "...................... production".

10 The initials TQM stand for T...................... Q...................... M......................

11 Market research which uses existing data is called .... research.

12 The process of removing layers of hierarchy in an organisation is called d......................

13 A pay system in which individuals are paid according to how many units they produce is called ....

14 The training individuals receive when they first join an organisation is called .... training

15 Using a low price to undercut the competition and force them out the market is called .... pricing.

What did you score?
Now check your answers, giving yourself one mark for each one correct.
If you scored:

12–15 marks	This is a good score and suggests you know all the different areas of the specification quite well. Congratulations! You need to look at any questions you got wrong, just to fill in any gaps, but you seem to know the material well.
8–11 marks	This is quite a good score and suggests you have a good grasp of many areas of the specification. However there are obviously still some gaps. Look over the questions you got wrong and work through those units again.
47 marks	This is rather a weak score. Look at the questions you got wrong to identify the areas you need to work through again, then work through those units a second time.
Less than 4 marks	This is obviously a disappointing score. Work your way through this book again and then have another go.

Review tests

Each of the following tests focuses on a particular area of the specification.

Once you have taken a test, check your answers. Give yourself one mark for each correct answer. If you scored:

12–15   **Congratulations! You clearly know this topic well.**

8–11   **This is quite a good score. It shows that you know some sections of this topic. However, there are some areas you need to revise.**

Less than 8 This is less than half marks. You obviously need to revise this topic again.

Review test 1: Marketing

1   What is meant by a market segment?
2   State two ways of measuring the size of a market.
3   Explain what is meant if a product is described as "price inelastic".
4   What is meant by a "Unique Selling Point"?
5   If a firm has a 40% market shares, what does this mean?
6   Explain what is meant by "market research".
7   What is meant by "primary data"?
8   Explain what is meant by a "marketing objective".
9   Explain what is meant by "price skimming".
10   Explain what is meant by the "product life cycle".
11   What is the Boston Matrix?
12   Explain what is meant by the term "income elastic"?
13   What is meant by a "confidence level" in market research?
14   What is meant by "price discrimination"?
15   Explain what is meant by a "loss leader".

Review test 2: Finance

1   What is meant by "variable costs"?
2   What is meant by the term "profit"?
3   State two internal sources of finance.
4   Selling price = £20 a unit; variable costs per unit = £15; fixed costs = £2000. What is the break-even level of output?
5   What is meant by a "budget"?
6   Explain what is meant by a favourable variance in budgeting.
7   What is a profit centre?
8   State two external sources of finance available to a company.
9   What is meant by the term "fixed costs"?
10   What is meant by the term "loss"?
11   Explain what is meant by "zero budgeting".
12   Explain what is meant by "working capital".
13   Explain two ways a firm might improve its cash flow.
14   Explain what is meant by a "debenture".
15   Explain what is meant by "contribution per unit".

Review test 3: People management

1   What is meant by "decentralisation"?
2   What is meant by the "span of control"?
3   What is meant by an "authoritarian style of management"?
4   What is meant by "empowerment"?
5   Explain one possible benefit of delegation.
6   Briefly outline Taylor's Scientific Management theory.
7   Explain one possible advantage of internal recruitment compared to external recruitment.
8   Explain what is meant by "job enrichment".
9   Explain what is meant by "induction training".
10   Explain what is meant by "management by objectives".
11   Explain what is meant by "corporate culture".
12   What is meant by "piecework"?
13   Explain McGregor's Theory X and Theory Y.
14   Explain Herzberg's "hygiene factors".
15   State the five levels of needs in Maslow's Hierarchy of Needs.

Review test 4: Operations

1   What is meant by "Just in Time production"?
2   What is meant by the term "capacity"?
3   What is meant by a "buffer stock"?
4   Explain what is meant by "capital intensive" production.
5   Explain what is meant by "job production".
6   What is meant by the term "diseconomies of scale"?
7   What is meant by "flow production"?
8   What is meant by "benchmarking"?
9   What is meant by "simultaneous engineering"?
10   Explain what is meant by "kaizen".
11   What is meant by "lean production"?
12   What is meant by "opportunity cost"?
13   What is meant by "excess capacity"?
14   What is meant by "productivity"?
15   What is "Total Quality Management"?

Review test 5: External influences

1   What is meant by "cyclical unemployment"?
2   What is meant by "social responsibility"?
3   Explain what is meant by the "business cycle".
4   Explain what is meant by "interest rates".
5   Explain what is meant by "employment laws".
6   What is capacity shortage?
7   What is meant by "exchange rate"?
8   What is the Retail Price Index?
9   What is deflation?
10   What is "structural unemployment"?
11   What is meant by "business ethics"?
12   What is a stakeholder?
13   What is the likely impact of higher interest rates on the demand for housing?
14   What is one possible cause of inflation?
15   State one consumer protection law.

Review test 6: Objectives and strategy

1   What is meant by a "plc"?
2   What is meant by SWOT analysis?
3   Explain what is meant by an "objective".
4   Explain what is meant by a "strategy".
5   Is manufacturing in the secondary or the tertiary sector of the economy?
6   Is farming in the primary or secondary sector of the economy?
7   What is a corporate aim?
8   What is meant by the "divorce between ownership and control"?
9   What is meant by "ltd"?
10   What is a sole trader?
11   What is a patent?
12   Explain what is meant by limited liability.
13   State two possible business objectives.
14   State four possible stakeholder groups in a business.
15   Who owns a company?

1 Marketing

1.1 Marketing analysis

Maths questions

1 £6 × 25 000 = £150 000

2 Market share = $\dfrac{120\,000}{600\,000} \times 100 = 20\%$

3 Market has increased by £100 000.

Increase = $\dfrac{£100\,000}{£300\,000} \times 100 = 33\frac{1}{3}\%$

4 a After 1 year: $\dfrac{5}{100} \times £400\,000 = £20\,000$

Market will be worth £400 000 + £20 000 = £420 000

b After 2 years: $\dfrac{5}{100} \times 420\,000 = £21\,000$

Market will be worth £441 000

5 Market share is $\dfrac{20}{100} \times £200\,000 = £40\,000$

If market grows by 50% it will grow by:

$\dfrac{50}{100} \times £200\,000 = £100\,000$

The new market is worth £200 000 + £100 000 = £300 000

So market share is $\dfrac{£40\,000}{£300\,000} \times 100 = 13.3\%$

Diagram questions

1 a Brand A has 25% ($\frac{1}{4}$) of the market.

25% = £160m so 1% = $\dfrac{160}{25} = £6.4m$

100% = 6.4m × 100 = £640m
Brand A has 25%; so A + C = 25% + 62% = 87%.
So Brand B has 100% − 87% = 13%

c Value of sales of Brand B: $\dfrac{13}{100} \times £640m = £83.2m$

d The market is worth
£640m × 2 = £1280.
Brand A will now have
12.5% ($\frac{1}{8}$) of the
market $\left(\dfrac{£160m}{£1280m}\right)$.

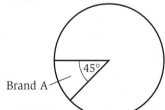

Brand A   45°

2 a Market has grown by
£80m − £50m = £30m.
This is $\dfrac{30}{50} \times 100 = 60\%$

b $\dfrac{25}{100} \times £80m = £20m$. Sales will be £80m + £20m = £100m

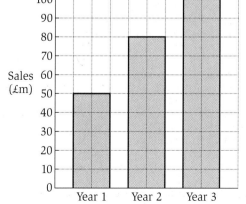

c 5% of year 3 market is $\dfrac{5}{100} \times £100m = £5m$

Quick questions

1 False. There is a 95% chance that the research results are right (regardless of whether they predict success or not).

2 Market segmentation

3 Secondary data

4 True

5 Slower and more expensive

6 False

7 Quota sample

8 Qualitative research

9 Primary research, because these names won't have been researched before

10 Declining market. Because to sell more, sales must come from other firms.

11 $\dfrac{\text{Coca Cola sales}}{\text{Total sales of soft drinks in the UK}} \times 100$

12 A low share of a large market may be worth more than a high share of a small market, e.g. 10% of a £600 m market is worth more than 50% of a £20 m market.

13 Costs may be increasing faster than revenue

14 By volume of sales.
By value of sales.

15 Slow rate. Because growth has already occurred. If sales are £100, 10% growth only means £10 of sales; if sales are £100m, 10% growth means an additional £10m.

Your chance to mark: examiner's comments

This candidate thinks carefully about the context of the question – it is focused very clearly on the magazine market. The arguments are developed quite effectively – there is a chain of argument (more targeted writing, more customer loyalty and possibly higher profits). The candidate also relates to market conditions and shows judgement, recognising that the need to "get it right" is even more important in a highly competitive market.

**Mark: Content: – 2/2 Application: – 2/2 Analysis: – 3/3
Evaluation: – 2/3 Total: – 9 /10**

1.2 Marketing strategy

Maths questions

1 $\dfrac{40}{100} \times 80\,000 = 32\,000$ units

2 Inflows: £3m × 2.2 = £6.6m
Outflows: £2.6m + £2.8m = £5.4m
Net cash flow = £6.6m – £5.4m = £1.2m

3 $\dfrac{400}{2000} \times 100 = 20\%$

4 Entering maturity – the growth of sales is slowing.

Diagram questions

1

		High	Star	Question mark
Rate of market growth (%)	Low		Cash cow	Dog
			High	Low

Relative market share

Answers

2 a

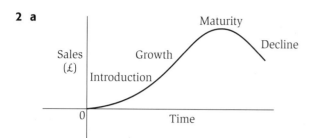

b typewriters: decline
Mars bars: maturity
videophones: introduction
DVDs: growth

c

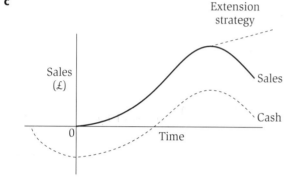

d

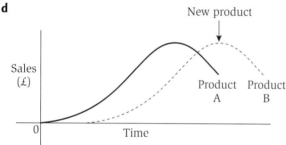

Quick questions

1 Marketing objective
2 Marketing strategy
3 Time
4 Adding value
5 False. The axes are market share and market growth
6 Growth
7 High market share in a slow growing market
8 Question mark
9 Low market share in a slow growing market
10 True
11 Low: because sales are low
12 An extension strategy
13 Product portfolio analysis
14 Determinism
15 High market share in a fast growing market

Your chance to mark: examiner's comments

This is a very general answer which completely ignores the context. There is no reference at all to the industry – the candidate could be writing about any market. Some ideas are

developed a little but there is no evaluation. To what extent are the advantages better than the disadvantages? Does a niche strategy make sense for someone in Jes's situation? What would make the advantages more or less important?

**Mark: Content: 2/2 Application: 0/2 Analysis: 3/3
Evaluation: 0/3 Total: 5/10**

1.3 Marketing planning

Maths questions

1 $\frac{25}{100} \times £4 = £1$. Selling price $= £4 + £1 = £5$
2 Unit cost $= \frac{£600}{300} = £2$ per unit.
$\frac{10}{100} \times £2 = £0.20$
Price $= £2 + £0.20 = £2.20$
3 Target: $\frac{40}{100} \times 2000 = 800$ outlets. Present number of outlets: 350. Therefore Marcham needs to increase the number of outlets by $800 - 350 = 450$.

Diagram questions

1 a

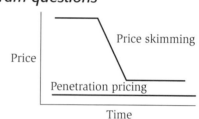

2 Marketing objective, marketing strategy, marketing planning

Quick questions

1 True
2 Penetration pricing
3 False
4 The cost per unit
5 Price taker
6 £60; cost-plus pricing
7 Promotion
8 False. Below the line
9 Price discrimination
10 Distribution target
11 Marketing objective
12 Few competitors. Individuals may pay more because they have few alternatives
13 Predatory pricing
14 Large scale. Use a low price to generate high sales and benefit from lower unit costs.
15 True

Your chance to mark: examiner's comments

This is a very evaluative answer throughout. The candidate is clearly thinking about this specific business with appropriate recommendations on how and where to promote the business. It also questions the usefulness of some types of promotion, recognising that "it depends".

**Mark: Content: 2/2 Application: 2/2 Analysis: 2/3
Evaluation: 3/3 Total: 9/10**

1.4 Elasticity of demand

Maths questions

1 a $\dfrac{100}{300} \times 100 = +33.3\%$

b $-\dfrac{1}{5} \times 100 = -20\%$

c $\dfrac{+33.3}{-20} = -1.67$

d Price elastic: the change in quantity demanded is greater than the change in price.

e £5 × 300 = £1500

f £4 × 400 = £1600

g When demand is price elastic, a cut in price leads to an increase in revenue.

2 a $\dfrac{10\,000}{50\,000} \times 100 = +20\%$

b $\dfrac{£2000}{£20\,000} \times 100 = +10\%$

c $\dfrac{+20}{+10} = +2$

Elastic, because the increase in demand is greater than the increase in income.

d £15 000 × 50 000 = £750 000 000

e £15 000 × 60 000 = £900 000 000

3 The price has fallen 10%. The price elasticity is –2. This means the change in quantity demanded will be 2 times the change in price (because the value is 2) and in the opposite direction (because it is a negative answer).

So change in sales will be $-2 \times -10\% = +20\%$ i.e. sales will increase by 20%.

4 The income elasticity is + 0.5. This means the change in quantity demanded will be 0.5 times the change in income (because the value is 0.5) and in the same direction (because the answer is positive).

Sales increase by $+0.5 \times +10\% = +5\%$

Diagram questions

1

Change in quantity demanded (units)	Change in price (£)	% change in quantity demanded	% change in price	Price elasticity of demand	Price elastic or inelastic
100 to 150	10 to 9	$+\dfrac{50}{100} \times 100$ $= +50\%$	$-\dfrac{1}{10} \times 100$ $= -10\%$	$\dfrac{+50}{-10} = -5$	Elastic
40 to 50	5 to 3	$+\dfrac{10}{40} \times 100$ $= +25\%$	$-\dfrac{2}{5} \times 100$ $= -40\%$	$\dfrac{+25}{-40} = -0.625$	Inelastic
20 to 22 (a change of +10%)	8 to 4	+10%	$-\dfrac{4}{8} \times 100$ $= -50\%$	$\dfrac{+10}{-50} = -0.2$	Inelastic
200 to 160 (i.e. −20%)	50 to 55 (i.e. +10%)	−20%	+10%	−2	Elastic

2

Change in quantity demanded (units)	Change in price (£)	Price elasticity	Elastic or inelastic	Old revenue	New revenue	Comment
400 to 480 $= \dfrac{80}{400} \times 100$ $= +20\%$	£10 to £9 $= -\dfrac{1}{10} \times 100$ $= -10\%$	$\dfrac{+20}{-10} = -2$	Elastic	400 × £10 = £4000	480 × £9 = £4320	Price elastic; lowering price increases revenue
400 to 420 $= +5\%$	£10 to £8 $= -20\%$	$\dfrac{+5}{-20}$ $= -0.25$	Inelastic	400 × £10 = £4000	420 × £8 = £3360	Price inelastic; lowering price decreases revenue
400 to 390 $= -2.5\%$	£10 to £15 $= +50\%$	$\dfrac{-2.5}{50}$ $= -0.05$	Inelastic	400 × £10 = £4000	390 × £15 = £5850	Price inelastic; increasing price increases revenue

Answers

Quick questions

1 Price elasticity of demand.
2 Income elasticity of demand.
3 Greater than 1
4 Less than 1
5 False. There may be a change in demand, but the percentage change in demand is less than the percentage change in price.
6 False. Income elasticity measures the impact of *income* changes on demand, not price changes.
7 $\dfrac{1}{-10} \times 100 = -10\%$
8 $\dfrac{1}{9} \times 100 = 11.11\%$
9 $\dfrac{+20\%}{+10\%} = +2$
10 $\dfrac{+10\%}{-50\%} = -0.2$
11 False. Price elastic, the value (ignoring the sign) is bigger than 1.
12 True
13 False: revenue decreases.
14 Low price elasticity and high income elasticity.
15 Low price elasticity and low income elasticity.

Your chance to mark: examiner's comments

A very good answer. It shows a good understanding of the concept and highlights two important factors: the perception of the car and who is paying. It analyses these factors quite well, providing an effective response.

Mark: Content: – 2/2 Application: – 2/2 Analysis: – 2/3
Total: – 6/7

2 Accounting and finance

2.1 Cost, profit and break-even analysis

Maths questions

1 **a** Contribution per unit = £10

b Break-even $= \dfrac{£10\,000}{£10} = 1000$ units

2 At an output of 2000:
Variable costs = £4000
Total costs = Fixed costs + Variable costs = £19 000

3 **a** Total revenue: £12 × 5000 = £60 000

b Total costs: £30 000 + £4000 = £34 000

c Profit: Total revenue − Total costs = £26 000

4 **a** Contribution per unit:
Selling price per unit − Variable cost per unit =
£50 − £20 = £30

b Break-even output:

$$\dfrac{\text{Fixed costs}}{\text{Contribution per unit}} = \dfrac{£6000}{£30} = 200 \text{ units}$$

5

Output per week	Fixed costs (£)	Variable costs (£)	Total costs (£)	Total revenue (£)	Profit (£)
0	15 000	0	15 000	0	(15 000)
500	15 000	2500	17 500	10 000	(7500)
1000	15 000	5000	20 000	20 000	0
1500	15 000	7500	22 500	30 000	7500
2000	15 000	10 000	25 000	40 000	15 000

Diagram questions

1

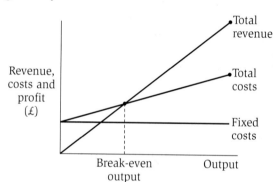

2

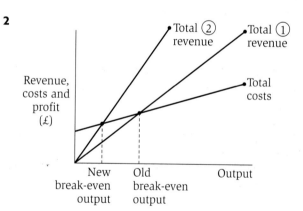

3

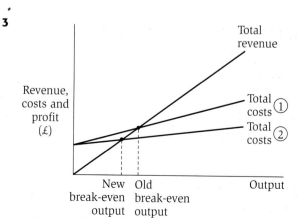

4

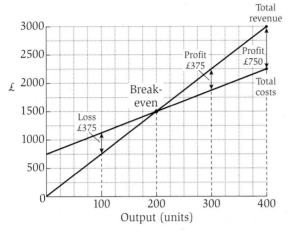

Quick questions

1 True
2 False: it occurs when Total revenue = Total costs
3 Total revenue = Price × Quantity sold
4 Total cost = Fixed costs + Variable costs
5 The contribution per unit = Selling price − Variable cost per unit
6 Profit = Total revenue − Total costs
7 Increase
8 Decrease
9 True
10 True
11 False, it will change the total revenue line
12 Increase
13 False, they do change, but not with output.
14 False, they can be variable
15 Overheads

Your chance to mark: examiner's comments

A rather brief answer, but nevertheless it shows an understanding of the concept. Two ways of reducing break-even are identified correctly. The idea of cutting costs is explored a little and some attempt is made to place it in the context of football.

Mark: Content: 2/2 Application: 1/2 Analysis: 2/3 Total: 5/7

2.2 Cash flow and finance

Maths questions

1

	January	February	March	April
Opening balance	200	210	230	220
Cash inflows	50	70	50	50
Cash outflows	40	50	60	80
Net cash flows (inflows – outflows)	10	20	(10)	(30)
Closing balance	210	230	220	190

Diagram questions

1

Internal	External
c	a
d	b

Quick questions

1 False – one vote per share
2 False – it is external
3 True
4 Overdraft
5 Sale and leaseback
6 False – debenture holders do not own the company; they do not have a vote
7 Dividends
8 c
9 **a** £50
   b Cash in: £0 (sold on credit)
   Cash out: £150
   Net cash flow: (£150)
10 c
11 Factoring
12 Working capital
13 True
14 Dividends
15 **b** Overdraft

Your chance to mark: examiner's comments

A good answer that considers two relevant issues – the credit period to customers and the payment period to suppliers. It rightly considers the reaction of both groups and highlights that what may seem a good idea might actually lead to more problems in the long term. A relevant, thoughtful answer, although it could have referred more to the industry or the small firms involved.

Mark: Content: 2/2 Application: 1/2 Analysis: 3/3 Evaluation: 3/3 Total: 9/10

2.3 Budgeting, cost centres and profit centres

Maths questions

1

Item	Budgeted figures (£)	Actual figures (£)	Variance (£)
Sales revenue	20 000	15 000	5000 adverse
Labour costs	5000	3000	2000 favourable
Material costs	1000	2000	1000 adverse
Other costs	2500	2500	0
Profit	11 500	7500	4000 adverse

Answers

2

Item	Budgeted figure	Actual figure	Variance
Sales revenue	£40 000	£44 000	£4000 favourable
Labour costs	£8000	£10 000	£2000 adverse
Material costs	£20 000	£18 000	£2000 favourable
Profit	£12 000	£16 000	£4000 favourable

3

Item	Budgeted figure	Actual figure	Variance
Sales revenue	£12 000	£13 000	£1000 favourable
Labour costs	£4000	£4800	£800 adverse
Material costs	£6000	£4700	£1300 favourable
Profit	£2000	£3500	£1500 favourable

Diagram questions

1

Adverse variance	Favourable variance
a	b
c	e
d	f

2

	True	False
This year's budget must always be bigger than last year's.		✓
A profit centre involves measuring revenues as well as costs for a part of the business.	✓	
A budget involves setting a non-financial, qualitative target.		✓
A budget involves setting a financial, qualitative target.	✓	

Quick questions

1 Budget

2 False: it is used to plan for the future.

3 Adverse

4 False. Budgets are used internally; they are not shown to the government.

5 Favourable

6 False

7 False

8 Profit centre

9 Adverse

10 Favourable

11 False

12 True

13 True

14 False

15 Cost centre – it does not generate revenue.

2.4 Investment appraisal, balance sheets and profit and loss statements

Maths questions

1 a Payback

Project A

Initial outflow = £20m. After year 1 we have £10m, so we need £10m more. In year 2 inflow is £15m overall but for payback we only need £10m of this.

$\frac{10}{15} = \frac{2}{3}$, so in year 2 £10m is earned after

$\frac{2}{3} \times 12 = 8$ months

So the payback for project A is 1 year 8 months.

Project B

Initial outflow = £50m. After year 1 we have £40m so we need £10m more. In year 2 we earn £40m but we only need £10m of this.

$\frac{10}{40} = 0.25$

0.25×12 months = 3 months

Payback for project B is 1 year and 3 months.

Accounting Rate of Return (ARR)

Project A:

Total profit = (£10m + £15m + £13m) − £20m = £18m

Average annual profit $= \frac{18}{3} = $ £6m

ARR $= \frac{6}{20} \times 100 = 30\%$ p.a.

Project B:

Total profit = (£40m + £40m + £12m) − £50m = £42m

Average annual profit $= \frac{42}{3} = $ £14m

ARR $= \frac{14}{50} \times 100 = 28\%$ p.a.

b Project A has a higher rate of return but a slightly slower payback. This one would be chosen on financial grounds assuming the firm can afford to wait the extra few months to recover its initial investment. There may, of course, be qualitative factors that would lead to project B being chosen.

2 $\frac{20}{100} \times$ £50m = £10m

3 Working capital = Current assets − Current liabilities
= £100m − £40m = £60m

Diagram questions

1 Fixed assets: building, machinery, factory (**d**, **e**, **g**)
   Current assets: cash, debtors (**a**, **h**)
   Current liabilities: overdraft, tax due to be paid, creditors (**b**, **f**, **i**)
   Long term liabilities: long-term loan (**c**)

2 Current liabilities: £12m
   Issued share capital: £18m
   Capital employed: £50m

3 Revenue: £9m
   Operating profit: £1m

Quick questions

1 Appraisal
2 Payback
3 d
4 a
5 c
6 b
7 Short payback; high accounting (average) rate of return
8 Revenue − Costs
9 Retained profit
10 c
11 a
12 b
13 False. The share price will fluctuate with demand for the shares; people may think the assets of the firm are worth more (or less) than their stated value on the balance sheet.
14 c
15 b

Your chance to mark: examiner's comments

The candidate shows some knowledge here but limited analysis, and no evaluation. He or she has an understanding of the balance sheet and profit and loss and tries to relate them to the context of investing. Some of the statements are simplistic, for example you don't always want to invest in a firm with large assets – it may be better to invest in a firm with fewer assets at the moment but good opportunities for growth.

**Mark: Content: 2/2 Application: 2/2 Analysis: 1/3
         Evaluation: 0/3 Total: 5/10**

3 People in organisations

3.1 Management structure and organisation

Diagram questions

1 3 (Marketing manager, Production manager and Finance manager)
2 Functional
3 Matrix
4 3

Quick questions

1 Centralised
2 Consultation

3 Increase
4 Delayering
5 c
6 c
7 c
8 Kaizen
9 Management By Objectives
10 a
11 Matrix
12 Mission
13 Delegation
14 a To increase sales by 20% over 3 years.
       (It contains a clear target and time element.)
15 b

Your chance to mark: examiner's comments

A rather general beginning; after this the answer starts to evaluate, recognising that the impact of introducing such a system depends on how it is introduced. The answer then starts to relate to the specific question, referring to the issues of performance and staff leaving. A slightly oddly structured answer, but showing many of the skills needed.

**Mark: Content: 2/2 Application: 2/2 Analysis: 2/3
         Evaluation: 3/3 Total: 9/10**

3.2 Motivation

Diagram questions

1 (1) Physiological (2) Security/safety (3) Social (4) Esteem (5) Self-actualisation

2 Examples of Hygiene factors: basic pay; working conditions; rules and regulations; colleagues
   Examples of Motivators: authority; feedback; opportunities for advancement/promotion

3

Theory X	Theory Y
a	c
b	d
e	f

4 **a** Piecework
   b

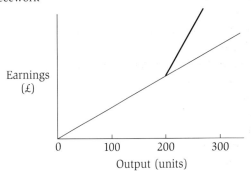

Quick questions

1 False. He believed that employees were motivated by money.
2 A fixed amount per year.
3 Authoritarian
4 Motivator
5 Theory Y

6 Democratic

7 Mayo

8 True

9 Piecework

10 **a** Basic pay

11 Scientific

12 Enrichment

13 Authoritarian

14 Security/safety

15 Esteem

Your chance to mark: examiner's comments

It is unusual for candidates to write about culture, so this is an interesting answer. This idea is discussed quite well. However, the student does not consider the context very much. In this case the manager is new, so will there be the same pressures on him to fit in with the culture? As the boss, he may want to change the culture.

Mark: Content: 1/2 Application: 0/2 Analysis: 1/3 Evaluation: 2/3 Total: 5/10

3.3 Human Resource Management
Maths questions

1 Labour turnover $= \dfrac{5}{80} \times 100 = 6.25\%$

2 **a** $\dfrac{25}{100} \times 400 = 100$ people leave on average each year.

b $100 \times £2000 = £200\,000$ p.a.

Diagram questions

1

Internal recruitment	External recruitment
a	b
d	c
e	f

2 Correct order: **gebfadc**

Quick questions

1 Human Resource Management

2 Internal

3 Induction

4 On the job

5 20% of 50 = 10 employees

6 Retirement

7 Dismissal

8 **d** A firm recruits employees from other firms

9 Off the job

10 Selection

11 Redundancy

12 Workforce planning

13 False. They are trained away from the job, but this training may be on company premises.

14 **a**

15 Offer more choice

Your chance to mark: examiner's comments

A rather general answer that makes relatively little reference to hotels. It does appreciate the importance of people and that

motivated staff can make a difference to business success, but it does not place the analysis in context. It refers to "production" and "defects" and "re-working items": this sounds very much like a standard manufacturing answer rather than an answer in the context of a hotel.

Other problems include the fact that this answer simply makes the case for HRM and refers only to motivation. HRM is much broader than this and also covers recruitment and selection and training, for example.

To "discuss" an issue it is important to show judgement. How important is HRM? What makes it more or less important?

Mark: Content: 1/2 Application: 1/2 Analysis: 2/3 Evaluation: 0/3 Total: 4/10

4 Operations management

4.1 Efficient production
Maths questions

1 **a** 5 claims per person per day.

b $\dfrac{£400}{5} = £80$ per claim

c 20% of 5 is $\dfrac{20}{100} \times 5 = 1$.

So new number of claims processed $= 5 + 1 = 6$ per day.

New labour costs $= \dfrac{£400}{6} = £66.67$ per claim

d The higher the productivity, the lower the labour cost per unit.

2 $\dfrac{120}{200} \times 100 = 60\%$

3 $80\% = 400$ units

$1\% = \dfrac{400}{80} = 5$ units

$100\% = 5 \times 100 = 500$ units

4 **a** $\dfrac{£4000}{500} = £8$ per unit

b 20% of 500 $= \dfrac{20}{100} \times 5 = 100$.

New output is $500 + 100 = 600$

10% of £4000 is £400, so new labour costs are £4000 + £400 = £4400.

New cost per unit $= \dfrac{£4400}{600} = £7.33$

5 **a** $\dfrac{\text{Total costs}}{\text{Output}}$

b $\dfrac{\text{Current output}}{\text{Maximum output}} \times 100$

c

Output	Total costs (£)	Unit costs (£)	Capacity utilisation (%)
100 000	200 000	2	20%
200 000	300 000	1.5	40%
300 000	360 000	1.2	60%
400 000	400 000	1	80%
500 000	480 000	0.96	100%

d Unit costs tend to fall as capacity utilisation increases.

6

Output (units)	Number of employees	Productivity (= output per employee) (units)	Total wage costs (£) (based on wage of £300 per week)	Labour Cost per unit (£) $\left(= \dfrac{\text{Total wages}}{\text{Output}}\right)$
100	10	10	3000	30
300	15	20	4500	15
500	20	25	6000	12
900	30	30	9000	10
1000	50	20	15 000	15

b As productivity increases, the labour cost per unit falls.

7

Capacity (units)	Output (units)	Capacity utilisation (%)	Fixed costs (£)	Fixed costs per unit (£) $\left(\dfrac{\text{Fixed costs}}{\text{Output}}\right)$
200	50	25	1000	20
200	100	50	1000	10
200	150	75	1000	6.67
200	200	100	1000	5

Diagram questions

1

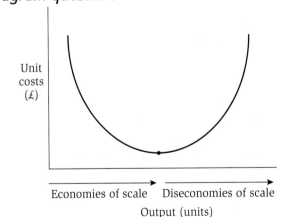

Unit costs (£)

Economies of scale → ← Diseconomies of scale

Output (units)

2 Job production: **a, e, f**
Flow production: **b, c, d**

Quick questions

1 b The output of a firm in relation to the inputs used up.
2 False. You could simply be making the same output with fewer people.
3 False. Economies of scale measure the unit cost. This falls, but the total cost may still be increasing.
4 Rationalisation
5 Job production
6 True
7 False – it is capital intensive.
8 Capacity

9 Flow production
10 c A firm is producing less than its maximum output.
11 Capital intensive
12 True
13 Low capacity utilisation
14 False. The output may not sell.
15 Capacity utilisation

Your chance to mark: examiner's comments

This is a weak answer for various reasons.
a The candidate shows some understanding of economies of scale but this is not entirely accurate – it should refer to "unit costs" not "costs".
b There is no attempt to relate the answer to a restaurant (so no application).
c The answer identifies a couple of types of economies of scale, but these are not analysed.
Overall, very disappointing.
Mark: Content: 1/2 Application: 0/2 Analysis: 0/3
      Total: 1/7

4.2 Controlling operations

Diagram questions

1 a 300 units
   b 200 units
   c 1 week
   d 500 units
   e 300 units
   f 100 units
2 Usage rate increased, e.g. due to extra demand.
3 e.g.
   ■ A failure to re-order
   ■ Materials ordered did not turn up, perhaps due to problems with supplier.

Quick questions

1 Benchmarking
2 Quality control
3 ISO 9000
4 Buffer
5 Lead time
6 Total Quality Management
7 d
8 Motivator
9 Opportunity cost
10 Lower
11 Wastage
12 Rotation
13 c Increase administration costs
14 False. The award is given if the firm sets targets and meets them, but does not judge whether the product itself is good quality (the targets could be easy to hit).
15 Increases

Your chance to mark: examiner's comments

A good answer that is quite evaluative. The candidate recognises there may not be a "right" answer – it depends! He

Answers

or she highlights the fact that it may depend on the product and there may be factors that actually conflict with each other.

Mark: Content: 2/2 Application: 2/2 Analysis: 3/3 Evaluation: 2/3 Total: 9/10

4.3 Lean production

Maths questions

1 5% of 50p is $\dfrac{5}{100} \times 50 = 2.5\text{p}$

On 6000 units a day, savings are $6000 \times 2.5 = 15\,000\text{p} = £150$ per day

2 Total stockholding is £2 000 000

5% interest is $\dfrac{5}{100} \times £2\,000\,000 = £100\,000$

Interest lost in one year is £100 000

Diagram questions

1 b

2

	High	Low
Stocks levels	◯	✓
Number of orders of stocks	✓	◯
Amount ordered each time	◯	✓
Desired lead time	◯	✓
Flexibility	✓	◯
Waste levels	◯	✓
Number of deliveries of supplies	✓	◯

Quick questions

1 c Produces items to order
2 Simultaneous engineering
3 False
4 Lean production
5 Low
6 Democratic
7 c The stockholding costs are high.
8 c Innovation is rapid.
9 d High stocks
10 b Suppliers are unreliable.
11 False. It aims for small developments.
12 Low
13 Motivator
14 Self-actualisation
15 Mayo

Your chance to mark: examiner's comments

The first sentence shows an understanding of the concept. The answer then relates to a leisure centre quite effectively. It rightly identifies the various demands on people's time and

that a leisure centre is only one option. The development of the argument is reasonable and highlights the importance of the need to improve (because everyone else is!).

Mark: Content: 2/2 Application: 2/2 Analysis: 3/3 Total: 7/7

5 External environment, objectives and strategy

5.1 External influences: economic and competitive environment

Maths questions

1 a i $\dfrac{-25}{500} \times 100 = -5\%$

ii $\dfrac{-25}{475} \times 100 = -5.26\%$

b Recession, because income is falling.

2 a Increase from 100 to 107 = 7%

b $\dfrac{2}{105} \times 100 = 1.9\%$

Diagram questions

1 d

2

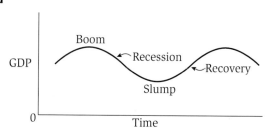

3 a Prices are rising but at a slower rate.
b Year 6 when prices are falling (negative growth).

Quick questions

1 c
2 Appreciated
3 Business cycle
4 d
5 Low
6 Tertiary sector
7 Cyclical unemployment
8 b
9 Gross Domestic Product
10 Deflation
11 a
12 c
13 Retail Price Index
14 Exporters, because it will be cheaper for foreigners to buy the currency, and therefore the country's goods and services.
15 The Monetary Policy Committee

Your chance to mark: examiner's comments

A good answer, in which the candidate clearly analyses the issues in the context of the product in the question and also evaluates well. The candidate shows a good understanding of interest rates but also recognises that the impact depends on a number of factors.

Mark: Content: 2/2 Application: 2/2 Analysis: 3/3 Evaluation: 3/3 Total: 10/10

5.2 External influences: political, social and technological environment

Diagram questions

1

Consumer law	Competition law	Health and Safety law
a	c	b
e	f	d

2 Students, staff, community, government

3

Stakeholder group	Objective
Shareholder	b
Employees	a
Customers	d
Local community	c

4

	True	False
The Trade Descriptions Act is an employment law.		✓
A shareholder is a stakeholder of the business.	✓	
Monopolies are illegal in the UK.		✓
The UK has a minimum wage.	✓	
A monopoly must have 100% market share.		✓
Companies are owned by all their stakeholders.		✓
You have the right to insist a shop sells an item at the same price as its competitors.		✓

Quick questions

1 d

2 False. New technology can create new markets and new jobs.

3 c

4 d

5 c

6 c

7 False; the Competition Commission may investigate monopolies but they are not illegal

8 Cartel

9 b

10 a

11 b

12 b

13 b

14 c

15 Competition

Your chance to mark: examiner's comments

A one-sided view. It contains some relevant ideas and an understanding of the appeal of ethical behaviour. A better answer would consider the case against (how ethics might reduce profits) and demonstrate some overall judgements ("it depends on …"). There is no attempt to relate to a manufacturing context.

Mark: Content: 2/2 Application: 0/2 Analysis: 2/3 Evaluation: 1/3 Total: 5/10

5.3 Start ups and objectives

Diagram questions

1

Primary	Secondary	Tertiary
b	a	c
d	e	g
f	i	h

2

Sole trader	Company
a	b
d	c

3 Shareholders: The owners of the company
Board of Directors: Elected by the owners
Managers: Control the company on a day-to-day basis.

4

Private limited company	Public limited company
b	a
c	e
d	f

5

SWOT	Feature
Strength	c
Weakness	a
Opportunity	b
Threat	d

6

SWOT	Feature
Strength	d
Weakness	b
Opportunity	c
Threat	a

Answers

Quick questions

1 d
2 a
3 c
4 a Copyright
  b Patent
5 b
6 Secondary
7 Primary
8 Stakeholders
9 b
10 c
11 d
12 a
13 d
14 False
15 Privatisation

Your chance to mark: examiner's comments

This answer has a good structure, with three clear paragraphs (for, against and conclusion). It highlights the benefits of a business plan for her quite effectively, but also recognises its limitations. It also considers the value of planning by referring to the fact that Gheeta's estimates may not be accurate. Overall a strong answer, although limited application.

Mark: Content: 2/2 Application: 1/2 Analysis: 2/3
       Evaluation: 3/3 Total: 8/10

Tests covering the whole specification

Test 1

1 The sales of a brand or product relative to the overall sales in the market.
2 Introduction, growth, maturity, decline
3 Sale of assets, sale and leaseback, profits, working capital
4 An IOU sold by companies to raise finance.
5 Entrusting a subordinate with a task.
6 Authoritarian (or autocratic)
7 Physiological, safety/security, social, esteem, self-actualisation
8 Unit
9 Capacity
10 Boom, recession, slump, recovery
11 Retail Price Index
12 Limited liability
13 Cyclical
14 Patent
15 Strengths, weaknesses, opportunities, threats

Test 2

1 Primary
2 Price elasticity of demand =
$$\frac{\text{Percentage change in quantity demanded}}{\text{Percentage change in price}}$$
3 X
4 Taylor

5 Buffer
6 Flow
7 Interest rate
8 Exchange rate
9 Stakeholder
10 There is a difference between the actual figures and the budgeted figures, which in themselves would mean that the actual profit is bigger than the budgeted one. This could be because the actual revenue is higher than the budgeted revenue or because the actual costs are lower than the budgeted costs.
11 The number of people directly responsible to a superior.
12 Workforce planning
13 Just in time
14 Ethics
15 Inflation

Test 3

1 False. It means that there is a 95% chance that the research findings are accurate, whatever these findings are.
2 A change in income leads to a bigger percentage change in the quantity demanded.
3 This is the minimum level of output at which Total revenue = Total costs.
4 Issued shares, loans, overdrafts, factoring
5 There is a difference between the actual figures and the budgeted figures so that the actual profit is less than the budgeted profit.
6 Asking employees for their opinion.
7 Democratic
8 Y
9 Economies of scale
10 Capacity utilisation
11 Batch
12 Opportunity
13 Kaizen
14 Excess
15 Activities are undertaken at the same time to speed up the development time for a new product or process.

Test 4

1 Deflation
2 The day-to-day financial position of an organisation (Current assets − Current liabilities)
3 Hygiene, motivator
4 Shortage
5 False. Shareholders have limited liability.
6 False. It is a quantifiable target.
7 Lead
8 Benchmarking
9 Lean
10 Total Quality Management
11 Secondary
12 Delayering
13 Piecework
14 Induction
15 Predator

Review tests

Review test 1: Marketing

1 A group of similar needs and wants within a market.

2 By measuring the value of sales or the volume of sales.

3 This means the percentage change in quantity demanded is less than the initial percentage change in price.

4 This is a feature of a product's marketing that differentiates it from the competition in the eyes of the consumer.

5 This means that the sales of the firm's product(s) are equal to 40% of the total sales in the market.

6 Market research is the process of gathering, analysing and presenting data relevant to the marketing process.

7 This is information that has been gathered for the first time, e.g. via surveys.

8 This is a marketing target, e.g. to increase sales.

9 This is an approach to pricing in which the price is set at a high level when the product is first launched on to the market.

10 This model shows the sales of a product over time.

11 This is a method of product portfolio analysis that examines a firm's products in terms of their market share and the market growth.

12 This means that the demand for a product is not sensitive to income: the change in quantity demanded is less than the initial percentage change in income.

13 This is a measure of the reliability of the market research findings; a 95% confidence level means the results of the research are likely to be accurate 95 times out of 100.

14 This occurs when different prices are charged for the same product.

15 This occurs when some products are sold by a firm at a loss to generate more sales for other products. The low price of some products attracts customers into the store and hopefully they buy other products.

Review test 2: Finance

1 Costs that vary with output.

2 Profit occurs when revenue (or sales) is greater than costs.

3 Retained profits; sale of assets.

4 Contribution per unit = £20 − £15 = £5 a unit.
Breakeven = $\frac{£2000}{£5}$ = 400 units

5 A quantifiable financial target.

6 This means that the actual revenue is more than the budgeted revenue, or the actual costs are less than the budgeted costs.

7 This occurs when the revenues and costs of a particular division, department or product are measured to assess its profits.

8 Loans, debentures, sale of shares, overdraft.

9 Costs that do not vary with output.

10 This occurs when revenue is less than costs.

11 This occurs when the budget is set at zero as a starting point; all financial targets have to be justified each time.

12 This measures the day-to-day finance of the business (Current assets − Current liabilities).

13 By chasing up debtors, by delaying payments to suppliers, by offering incentives for cash payments.

14 A form of IOU; a business sells debentures and then repays over a period of time.

15 Selling price per unit − Variable cost per unit; this contributes towards fixed costs.

Review test 3: People management

1 The extent to which authority is dispersed throughout the organisation.

2 The number of subordinates directly responsible to a superior.

3 Occurs when managers tell employees what to do; associated with one-way communication.

4 Occurs when employees are given a high degree of control over their working lives, e.g. determining what has to be done and when.

5 It may motivate; it may make use of specialist skills; it may reduce superiors' workload, enabling better planning.

6 Involves developing the "one best way" of doing a job; this method developed scientifically, i.e. through observation, developing a new technique and measuring the results. It assumes employees are motivated by money and so respond to being shown how to improve their productivity and therefore their pay.

7 May be quicker to recruit; already have an insight into the employee's strengths and weaknesses.

8 Also called "vertical loading"; an employee is given greater authority and more challenging tasks.

9 This is the initial training an employee receives when starting at a business, e.g. introducing the individual to the firm, the job and colleagues.

10 A system of target setting at every level of the organisation to coordinate employees' actions.

11 The values, attitudes and beliefs of employees.

12 A payment system in which employees are paid according to the number of units produced.

13 Describes two types of managers: Theory X managers do not trust employees and believe they need controlling; Theory Y managers do trust employees and believe they respond to having more authority.

14 These are factors at work which prevent dissatisfaction but which do not actually motivate, e.g. basic pay, colleagues, company rules and policy.

15 Physiological, safety, security, esteem(ego), self-actualisation.

Review test 4: Operations

1 A method of production that produces to order and attempts to minimise stock levels.

2 The maximum output a firm can produce, given its resources.

3 The minimum level of output a firm wants to hold at any moment.

4 A method of production that involves high levels of machinery relative to labour, e.g. a production line process.

5 A flexible method of production that focuses on one-off products made to meet specific customer requirements.

Answers

6 Occurs when the unit costs increase as the scale of production increases.

7 A continuous production process in which items move directly from one stage of the process to another; suitable for large-scale production.

8 Occurs when a firm measures its performance in specific activities against the leading firms in this area.

9 Occurs when activities involved in developing a new product are undertaken at the same time, rather than one after another, to save time.

10 Occurs when an organisation seeks to improve continuously.

11 An approach that seeks to minimise all forms of waste within the organisation.

12 This is the benefit foregone by undertaking a particular activity, e.g. by holding stocks money is tied up which could be earning interest elsewhere.

13 Occurs when a firm is able to produce more than it is producing, given its resources.

14 This is a measure of output in relation to inputs, e.g. the output per worker.

15 An approach in which all employees are involved in improving quality in the organisation.

Review test 5: External influences

1 Occurs when employees lose their jobs because of a lack of demand throughout the economy.

2 The extent to which a firm accepts its obligations towards society in general.

3 Measures changes in Gross Domestic Product over time; this usually follows a pattern of boom, recession, slump and recovery.

4 The costs of borrowing money and the reward for saving.

5 Legislation that affects the terms and conditions of staff employment, e.g. preventing discrimination, setting a minimum wage.

6 Occurs when the amount a firm can produce with its given resources is less than the demand.

7 The price of one currency in terms of another, e.g. the number of euros it takes to buy a dollar.

8 This is a measure of inflation.

9 This occurs when prices are falling.

10 This occurs when employees lose their jobs because the nature of the economy has changed, i.e. their sector has become uncompetitive.

11 Refers to managers' decisions about what is the right or wrong behaviour in any given business situation.

12 Any group or individual that affects or is affected by the activities of a firm.

13 Higher interest rates will tend to encourage saving and reduce the desire to borrow; this is likely to reduce demand for housing.

14 May be caused by high levels of demand in an economy pulling up prices, or higher costs forcing firms to push up their prices.

15 Sales of Goods Act, Trade Descriptions Act, Weights and Measures Act.

Review test 6: Objectives and strategy

1 A public limited company

2 Strengths, Weaknesses, Opportunities and Threats

3 A quantifiable target.

4 A long-term plan set to achieve an objective.

5 Secondary.

6 Primary.

7 The overall direction of the organisation.

8 Occurs in companies when the owners (shareholders) are not the same as the people who control the business (the managers); this can lead to a conflict of objectives.

9 A private limited company.

10 An entrepreneur who runs his or her own business.

11 Legal protection for a new product or production process.

12 This limits the extent to which investors are liable for the organisation's liabilities, e.g. if they invest £100 they could lose this but no more.

13 Examples include: to increase profits, to increase sales, to grow, to survive, to innovate, within a given timescale.

14 Stakeholders include: employees, shareholders, the local residents, the suppliers, the government.

15 The shareholders.

Index